T5-CVQ-489

SYSTEM ADMINISTRATOR COLLECTION

UNIX® System V
NFS Administration

Edited by
Debra Herman

P T R Prentice Hall
Englewood Cliffs, New Jersey 07632

PRENTICE HALL OPEN SYSTEMS LIBRARY

Library of Congress Cataloging-in-Publication Data

UNIX System V NFS Administration/Debra Herman, editor
p. cm.
Includes index.
ISBN 0-13-016411-9
1. Operating systems (computers) 2. UNIX System V (Computer file)
3. Computer networks. I. Herman, Debra.
QA76.76.063U5521125 1993
005.7'13--dc20 92-44385
CIP

Editorial/production supervision: *Harriet Tellem*
Cover design: *Eloise Starkweather*
Manufacturing buyer: *Mary E. McCartney*
Acquisitons editor: *Phyllis Eve Bregman*
Cover art: *The Owl* (Miro). (From Superstock)

Published by P T R Prentice-Hall, Inc.
A Simon & Schuster Company
Englewood Cliffs, New Jersey 07632

The publisher offers discounts on this book when ordered in bulk quantities. For more information contact:

Corporate Sales Department
P T R Prentice Hall
113 Sylvan Avenue
Enlgewood Cliffs, NJ 07632

Phone: 201-592-2863
Fax: 201-592-2249

Printed in the United States of America
10 9 8 7 6 5 4 3 2 1

ISBN 0-13-016411-9

Prentice-Hall International (UK) Limited, *London*
Prentice-Hall of Australia Pty. Limited, *Sydney*
Prentice-Hall Canada Inc., *Toronto*
Prentice-Hall Hispanoamericana, S.A.,
Prentice-Hall of India Private Limited, *New Delhi*
Prentice-Hall of Japan, Inc., *Tokyo*
Simon & Schuster Asia Pte. Ltd., *Singapore*
Editor Prentice-Hall do Brasil, Ltda., *Rio de Janeiro*

Table of Contents

Preface — ix

About this Book — ix
Organization — x
Conventions Used — xi

Chapter 1: Introduction — 1

About NFS — 1
The NFS File Sharing Model — 1
NFS Advantages — 4
NFS Administration — 6

Chapter 2: Using NFS — 7

Introduction — 7
Installing NFS — 7
Starting and Stopping NFS Operation — 8
Sharing and Unsharing Resources — 9
Mounting Resources — 18
Obtaining Information — 23

Chapter 3: Handling NFS Problems — 27

Introduction — 27
The NFS Daemons — 28
An Overview of the Mount Process — 29
Determining Where NFS Service Has Failed — 31
Fixing Hung Programs — 36

Chapter 4: The Automounter 41

Introduction 41
How the Automounter Works 42
Preparing the Maps 43
Invoking the Automounter 56
Modifying the Maps 58
Updating the Mount Table 58
Handling Automounter Problems 58

Chapter 5: The sysadm Interface 63

Introduction 63
Using sysadm 64
Setting Up NFS 64
Starting and Stopping NFS 65
Local Resource Sharing 66
Remote Resource Mounting 67

Chapter 6: Secure NFS 69

Introduction 69
An Overview of Secure RPC 70
Administering Secure NFS 75
Important Considerations 78

Chapter 7: The Network Lock Manager 81

Introduction 81
The Locking Protocol 84
The Network Status Monitor 86

Chapter 8: Remote Services 87

Introduction 87
Copying Files Between Machines 88
Executing Commands Remotely 92
Transferring Files Between Machines 94
Logging In to Remote Machines 101
Obtaining Information 109

Chapter 9: The NIS Service 113

Introduction 113
The NIS Environment 114
Setting Up the NIS Service 120
Administering NIS Maps 135
Adding a New NIS Server 142
Handling NIS Problems 145
Turning Off NIS Services 152

Glossary 153

Index 157

List of Figures

1-1 Mounting a Remote Resource 3
1-2 Selective File Sharing 4

2-1 Sharing Resources on a Regular Basis 13

3-1 Checking `mountd` Daemons 32
3-2 Checking `nfsd` Daemons 32
3-3 Checking `biod` Daemons 32
3-4 Sample `rpcinfo` 34

4-1 A Symbolic Link from the Requested to Actual Mount Point 42
4-2 Sample Master Map 45
4-3 Typical Direct Map 47
4-4 Typical Indirect Map 48
4-5 Map Entry Describing Multiple Mounts 49
4-6 Another Map Entry with Multiple Mounts 49
4-7 Map with Different Options and More than One Server 50
4-8 Specifying Subdirectory in Master Map 52
4-9 Using String Substitutions to Simplify Map Entries 53
4-10 Substituting Ampersand for Key 53
4-11 Server Name the Same as Key 54
4-12 Specifying Subdirectory in Master Map 54
4-13 Using the Asterisk When All Map Entries Have the Same Format 54

5-1 NFS System Setup Screen 65
5-2 NFS System Control Screen 66
5-3 Local Resource Sharing Management Screen 67
5-4 Remote Resource Access Management 68

6-1 Locking Service Architecture 83

7-1 Sample `ftp` Login 95
7-2 Setting Up a Machine to Allow Anonymous `ftp` 96
7-3 Anonymous `ftp` Session 97
7-4 Transferring Files with `ftp` 98
7-5 Transferring a File with `mget` and `mput` 99
7-6 Sample `rlogin` Session 102
7-7 Aborting an `rlogin` Connection 104
7-8 Disconnecting an Intermediate `rlogin` 105
7-9 Suspending a Remote Connection 105
7-10 Establishing a Remote Connection with `telnet` 107
7-11 Suspending a `telnet` Connection 108
7-12 Aborting a `telnet` Connection 109
7-13 Example `finger` Session 110

8-1 The Relationship Between Master, Slave, and Client Servers 118
8-2 `chkey` Session 122
8-3 `auto.master` Map File 123
8-4 `auto.home` Map File 124
8-5 `auto.direct` Map File 124
8-6 Default Makefile 126
8-7 Automounter Makefile 129
8-8 Bringing Master Server to Run Level Allowing NIS Services to Run 131
8-9 Building a NIS Map from Standard Input 138
8-10 Updating NIS Maps with Shell Scripts 140
8-11 Output from `rpcbind` 149
8-12 Transferring a NIS Map File 151
8-13 Output from `rpcinfo` 152

Preface

❑ About this Book

This book explains how to administer the System V Release 4.0 implementation of Sun's NFS® distributed computing file system. It explains how the NFS system works and describes the procedures for sharing resources across a network. The special NFS services, the automounter, secure NFS, and the Network Lock Manager are described, as is the simplified `sysadm` menu-driven interface to basic NFS operation. The remote user services supported by NFS are explained, as is the NIS distributed name service.

In most UNIX® system environments, a shareable file hierarchy corresponds to a file system or to a portion of a file system. Since NFS works across operating systems, and the concept of a file system may be meaningless in other, non-UNIX system environments, the term *resource* is used throughout this book to refer to a file or file hierarchy that can be shared and mounted over NFS.

Audience

UNIX System V NFS Administration is for system administrators who are setting up and maintaining distributed file systems using NFS on UNIX System V systems, and for users of the remote services provided by NFS.

This book explains how to set up a machine to share local resources with other machines on a network, and how to mount remote resource made available by other systems. If you are administering a machine that will mount but not share resources, you may choose to focus on those sections that describe the mounting of resources and to skip those that describe the sharing of resources.

❑ Organization

This book is organized as follows:

- ▲ "Introduction" describes the key concepts underlying NFS and highlights its most important features.
- ▲ "Using NFS" describes how to install NFS, start NFS operation, share and mount resources, get information about shared resources, and handle any problems that might occur.
- ▲ "Handling NFS Problems" provides general information needed to understand possible NFS problems and gives strategies for dealing with services failures and hung programs.
- ▲ "The Automounter" explains how to use the automatic mounting facility of NFS.
- ▲ "The `sysadm` Interface," explains how to set up and administer NFS using a menu-driven interface.
- ▲ "Secure NFS" describes the NFS options that provide for authentication, encryption, and other security measures.
- ▲ "The Network Lock Manager" describes the system calls used to prevent multiple processes from modifying the same file at the same time.
- ▲ "Remote Services" explains how to copy remote files, execute commands on a remote machine, log in to a remote machine, transfer files between machines, and obtain information about other machines or users on a network.
- ▲ "The NIS Service" describes the distributed name service used to identify network computing services and to provide a uniform, network-wide storage and retrieval method.
- ▲ "Glossary" defines the special terms used in this book.

❑ Conventions Used

The following formatting conventions are used in documenting command syntax and in making text and examples more easily understood:

- ▲ Items enclosed in square brackets ([]) are optional.

  `[OKTOSKIP]`

- ▲ A vertical bar (|) separates items that are alternatives.

  `tweedledee | tweedledum`

- ▲ Items shown in the typeface `Courier` represent text you enter at the command line or in a file, or output from the UNIX shell.

  `$ logout`

- ▲ Items shown in *italic* text are names that must be expanded to their actual value before being entered at the command line or typed into a file. `rlogin` *hostname* might actually be written:

  `$rlogin neptune`

- ▲ An asterisk next to an item, as in *asmanyasdesired** indicates that item can be repeated zero or more times. `dfmounts [` *server* `]*` might actually be written:

  `$ dfmounts rose geranium lily`

- ▲ A backslash (\) at the end of a command line indicates that the command is continued on the line that follows. This is the case in the command line that follows:

```
$ share -F NFS -o ro, rw=lisa, dave, gordon \
/usr/local/lib/minutes.doc
```

- ▲ Collateral information appears in the text as notes.

Copying directories with `rcp` does not preserve ownership settings nor does it necessarily preserve permissions.

- ▲ Cautionary information appears in text as a warning.

Permitting root access to a server is inadvisable in all but the most trusting environments.

- Extended examples of interaction in the computer shell are shown in a screen intended to resemble a terminal window.

```
$ telnet mars
Trying...
Connected to mars
Escape Character is '^]'
```

- Parenthetical remarks are occasionally used to clarify the meaning of text shown in these screens. Such text will appear in italic type as shown below. The change of typeface indicates text that does not actually appear on your screen.

```
venus$ rlogin jupiter -l steve
Password (Type your password here)
Last login: Mon Oct 21 00:30:52 from venus
jupiter$
```

- To make clear whether a shell is local or remote, the screen prompts in the example above and in many of the examples that follow are shown in the form *hostname*`$`. To set your terminal to include the host name in the prompt, add the line shown to your `$HOME/.profile` file:

```
PS1="`hostname`$PS1"
```

The names of keys are shown in boldface when used in text. For example, the return key is shown as **Return**. The control key is abbreviated as **Ctrl** and generally appears with a hyphen and the name of a second key intended to be pressed simultaneously, as in, **Ctrl-Z**.

Related Reading

UNIX System V Release 4 Programmer's Guide: Networking Interfaces, UNIX System Laboratories, Prentice Hall, Englewood Cliffs, NJ, ISBN: 0-13-947078-6.

UNIX System V Release 4 Network User's and Administrator's Guide, UNIX System Laboratories, Prentice Hall, Englewood Cliffs, NJ, ISBN: 0-13-933813-6.

UNIX System V Release 4 System Administrator's Guide, UNIX System Laboratories, Prentice Hall, Englewood Cliffs, NJ: ISBN: 0-13-947086-7.

UNIX System V Release 4 User's Reference Manual/ System Administrator's Reference Manual (two volumes), UNIX System Laboratories, Prentice Hall, Englewood Cliffs, NJ: ISBN: Commands a-l: 0-13-951310-8; Commands m-z: 0-13-9511328-0.

Acknowledgments

This book is derived from information in the UNIX System V Release 4 and SV/386 Release 3.4 System Administrator's Guides and Reference Manuals, and on-line manual pages. While the material has been rearranged and reworked, expanded here and contracted there, it retains much of the flavor and many of the words of the original material.

Our thanks to Dorothy Chang, Elka Grisham, Dick Hamilton, and Bill Klinger from UNIX System Laboratories for their continuous support during this project. Thanks also to Phyllis Eve Bregman, my editor at Prentice Hall, and to Chi-Ti Chen, Mary Fox and John Van Dyk for reviewing the manuscript.

1

Introduction

❑ About NFS

NFS file sharing is used to make resources on a local system available to remote systems and, conversely, to access resources on remote systems from a local system. Using NFS, it possible to share individual files, file hierarchies, and entire file systems across a network.

NFS enables machines of different architectures running different operating systems to share resources across a network. It has been implemented on operating systems ranging from MS-DOS to VMS.

Operation in a heterogeneous environment is possible because NFS defines an abstract file system model. On each supported operating system, the NFS model is mapped into the local file system semantics. As a result, normal file system operations, such as read and write, operate in the same way that they operate on the local file system.

❑ The NFS File Sharing Model

System V file sharing employs a *client/server* model. A machine that wishes to share its file systems with other machines on a network acts as a *server*. Files are physically located on and managed by the server machine. A machine that wishes to access file systems that do not reside on its physical disk acts as a *client* of the server machine. Acting on behalf of its applications, the client makes requests to the server to access data in a file or to perform file manipulations. If desired, a single machine act as both a client and a server, sharing its local file systems and accessing remote file systems.

A server can support *diskless* clients, machines that have no local disks. A diskless client relies completely on the server for all its file storage. Since it has no file system to make available, a diskless client can act only as a client—never as a server.

Clients access files on a server by mounting that server's shared resources. When a client mounts a remote resource, it does not make a copy of the resource. Rather, the mounting process uses a series of remote procedure calls (RPC's) that enable the client to access the resource on the server's disk *as if* it were on its own disk. This transparency is the key to the usefulness of file sharing. Once mounted, remote file systems look like local file systems from a user or application perspective.

A server can offer any directory tree for access over the network. From the client's point of view, such a directory tree constitutes a file system. Once a remote file system is made available for sharing, an authorized client can mount that file system on any of its local directories. Once so mounted, the remote file system becomes a shared resource.

Special device files, as well as ordinary files, can be shared over NFS. Peripheral devices, such as modems and printers, cannot be shared.

When a local file system is mounted on a local mount point, the entire file system, starting at its root is mounted. When mounting a remote resource through NFS, it is not necessary to mount the entire file system. You can mount any directory or file in the directory tree, gaining access only to that directory or file and anything beneath it.

In Figure 1-1, Machine A has made its entire `/usr` file system available for sharing. If Machine B wants access only to those files and subdirectories in `/usr/man`, it can mount `/usr/man`, rather than `/usr`. Doing so results in nothing above `/usr/man` on Machine A appearing in Machine B's directory tree.

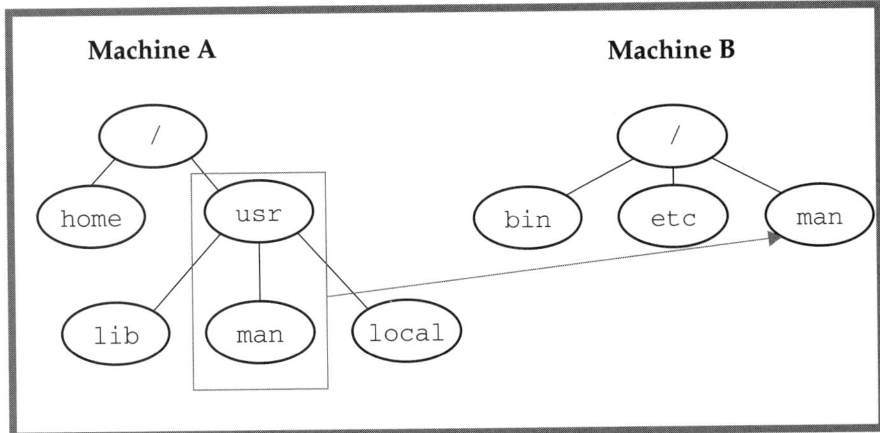

Figure 1-1: Mounting a Remote Resource

Machine A cannot share both /usr and /usr/man if both resources reside on the same disk partition. It is necessary to share /usr, allowing each network machine to decide whether to mount /usr or /usr/man. To mount a single file, it is necessary to mount the file on a directory. Once it is mounted, it cannot be removed (with rm) or moved to another directory (with mv). You can only unmount it.

Just as clients need not mount an entire file system, servers need not make all their files accessible to network clients. In Figure 1-2, the server makes the directory /public/tkit available for sharing. In contrast, the directory /public/tkit2 is not shared. When the client mounts /public/tkit on its local directory /usr/tools, the remote directory tree appears to be a directory tree under /usr/tools. Files in that tree can be accessed as though they were local. The files in /public/tkit2 are *not* accessible.

Figure 1-2: Selective File Sharing

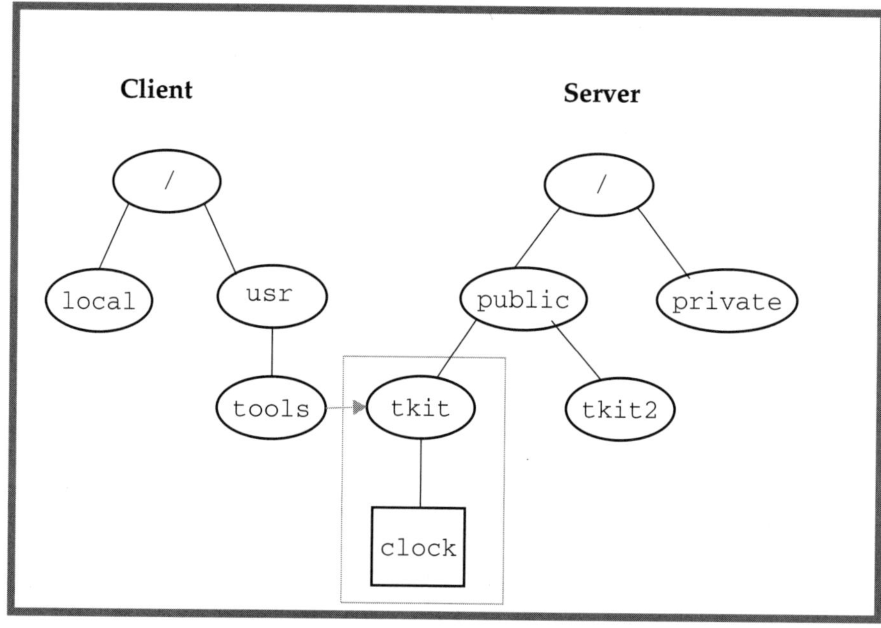

◆ ***Note*** A machine cannot share a file hierarchy that overlaps one that is already shared.

As an alternative to centralizing resources on a few servers, NFS files can be shared in a peer-to-peer manner. When a single computer runs out of capacity, additional computers can be added to a configuration. Resources can be moved to a new computers, while maintaining a consistent user view of the directory tree.

❑ NFS Advantages

With NFS, remote resources can be mounted anywhere in a local tree. This allows programs running on several different computers to have the same files and directory structure made available to them. Similarly, in an NFS environment, a large number of users can access a program as though it were on their local machines, when actually the program resides on a single resource server. This is a great benefit to users of small workstations, where disk space is at a premium. With remote resource access, the user can reach a much larger program repertoire than could fit on a private disk.

By having a resource reside physically on a single server, then distributing that resource throughout the network via file sharing, system administration is greatly simplified because

- Fewer copies of programs need to be maintained on the network
- The problems involved in performing backups for a number of machines dispersed over a wide geographical area are reduced. By keeping files in a single location, this task becomes comparable to backing up a single machine.

Centralizing files on a few file servers not only simplifies administration, it helps maintain the consistency of shared data files. When changes are made to a shared file, they become available to all users immediately. Allowing multiple machines to use the same files keeps storage costs down because machines share applications. Database consistency and reliability is enhanced because all users read the same set of files.

NFS provides good recovery prospects when file servers fail. NFS servers do not keep any state information about the clients accessing them. If a client crashes, the server is oblivious to it. If the server crashes, clients can either block until the server comes up or return an error after a time-out.

NFS takes advantage of a network locking facility called the Network Lock Manager. The lock manager supports the UNIX System V style of advisory and mandatory file and record locking.

NFS assumes global UID/GID space and provides an administrator with the ability to restrict which machines can access resources; to specify read-only access to shared directories; and to unshare a directory, causing client access to that directory to fail. For additional security, Secure NFS supports encrypted machine and user identification along with ID mapping.

Because NFS provides transparent access, within limits, NFS allows existing applications that do not attempt to use unsupported features to run without recompilation.

Release 4.0 standardizes the syntax of administrative commands to NFS, providing a uniform interface to distributed file systems. Options that handle file system-dependent functionality accommodate differences, while integrating common features. Older forms of commands remain available to provide compatibility with previous releases.

NFS is built on top of the Remote Procedure Call (RPC) facility, which requires the User Datagram Protocol (UDP) transport. UDP is a protocol in the TCP/IP protocol family.

❑ NFS Administration

The responsibilities of an NFS administrator depend on site requirements and the role of the administered machine on the network.

If you are responsible for all the machines on your local network, you are very likely be responsible for installing the software on every machine and determining the role of each machine on the network. This mean deciding which machines, if any, should be dedicated servers, which should act as both servers and clients, and which should be clients only.

If your site has a network administrator, and you are the administrator of a client-only machine, you most likely have responsibility only for mounting and unmounting remote resources on that machine.

Once initial NFS setup has taken place, maintaining a machine involves the following tasks:

- ▲ Starting and stopping NFS operation.
- ▲ Sharing and unsharing resources.
- ▲ Mounting and unmounting resources.
- ▲ Modifying administrative files to update the lists of resources a machine shares and/or mounts automatically.
- ▲ Checking the status of the network.
- ▲ Diagnosing and fixing NFS-related problems as they arise.
- ▲ Setting up maps to use the optional automatic mounting facility, called the automounter.
- ▲ Setting up the optional security features provided by Secure NFS.

2

Using NFS

❑ Introduction

This chapter provides basic information regarding NFS operation. More specifically, it discusses each of the following tasks:

- ▲ Installing NFS.
- ▲ Starting and stopping NFS operation.
- ▲ Sharing and unsharing resources.
- ▲ Mounting resources.
- ▲ Obtaining information about mounted or shared resources.

❑ Installing NFS

The Network File System software is packaged on floppy diskettes or cartridge tape and distributed with UNIX System V Release 4.0. If all the software in Release 4.0, NFS is installed on your system, NFS is already on your system. If not, you must install the following System V utilities before installing NFS:

- ▲ Remote Procedure Call (RPC) Utilities
- ▲ Network Support Utilities (NSU)
- ▲ Network Support Utilities
- ▲ Distributed File System Administration utilities (DFS) (optional).
- ▲ TCP/IP utilities.

Instructions for installing these utilities, as well as NFS, appear in the System V Release 4.0 *Release Notes.*

❑ Starting and Stopping NFS Operation

NFS automatically becomes operational whenever your system enters run level 3. This can happen in one of two ways. NFS operation can be started by entering the `init` command at the command line. Alternatively, NFS can be started *automatically* each time you reboot your system. If you set up automatic sharing and mounting, a predetermined set of resources is shared and/or mounted whenever you start NFS operation.

To start NFS from the command line, type

```
init 3
sh /etc/init.d/nfs start
```

To stop NFS operation, exit run level 3. When you do so, any the resources shared or mounted are automatically unshared or unmounted.

To stop NFS from the command line, type

```
sh /etc/init.d/nfs stop
```

❑ Sharing and Unsharing Resources

This section describes how to share resources by using NFS. It explains how to make a resource available for sharing with client machines and, when desired, how to stop sharing that resource.

The sharing and unsharing of resources can be controlled from the command line. Such an approach is appropriate for resources that are used intermittently or temporarily. Sharing from the command line is described in the next section. Sharing of resources can also be done automatically. This approach works best for resources needed on a regular basis. For additional information, see "Automatic Sharing" on page 15. A third possibility, sharing resources as-needed, is discussed in "The Automounter" on page 39.

Sharing and Unsharing Resources

The `share` and `shareall` commands make it possible to share resources. `share` makes a single resource available for sharing, `shareall` makes a group of resources available. The `unshare` and `unshareall` commands make it possible to end the sharing of one or more resources.

The `share` Command

The `share` command makes resources available for sharing. Use `share` at the command line when you want to share a resource for a brief period of time or when a resource is needed for sharing on an irregular basis.

The `share` command is located in `/usr/sbin` and has the form:

```
share [-F nfs] [-o specific-options] [-d description] pathname
```

where

`-F nfs`	indicates that the resource should be shared through NFS.
`-o` *specific-options*	is a comma-separated list of options that regulates how the resource is shared.

-d *description* — is a comment that describes the resource to be shared.

pathname — is the full name of the resource to be shared, starting at root (/).

If NFS is the only file sharing package installed on your machine, `nfs` is the default, and the `-F` option can be omitted.

The Specific Options For `share`

The *specific options* that can follow the `-o` flag are as follows:

`rw` — shares the resource read/write to all clients, except those specified under `ro=`.

`ro` — shares the resource read-only to all clients, except those specified under `rw=`.

`ro=`*client*`[:`*client*`]`* — shares the resource read-only to the listed clients (overriding `rw` for those clients only).

`rw=`*client*`[:`*client*`]`* — shares the resource read/write to the listed clients (overriding `ro` for those clients only).

`anon=`*uid* — specifies a new user identifier, *uid*, for "anonymous" users when accessing the resource. By default, anonymous users are mapped to username `nobody`, which has the user identifiers (UID) `UID_NOBODY`. User `nobody` has ordinary user privileges, not superuser privileges.

`root=`*host*`[:`*host*`]`* — allows a user from the specified host or hosts whose UID is `0` to access the resource as root; root users from all other hosts become `anon`. If this option is not specified, no user from any host is granted access to the resource as root.

`secure` — shares a resource, with additional user authentication required. See "Secure NFS" on page 67.

◆ ***Note*** An asterisk (*) indicates an item that can be repeated zero or more times. See "Conventions Used" on page xi.

In choosing specific options, you cannot specify both read-write (`rw`) and read-only (`ro`) without arguments as these are mutually exclusive choices. For the same reason, you cannot specify the same client in the `rw=` list and the `ro=` list. If no read/write option is specified, the default is read/write for all clients.

When using the option `root=` to grant root access to other hosts, be aware of that fact that such a choice has far reaching security implications. As a result, use this option with extreme caution. See "Accessing Shared Resources as Superuser" on page 16 for additional information.

In choosing specific options, you cannot specify both read/write (`rw`) and read-only (`ro`) without arguments, as these are mutually exclusive choices. For the same reason, you cannot specify the same client in the `rw=` list and the `ro=` list. If no read/write option is specified, then the default is read/write for all clients.

When using the option `root=` to grant access to other hosts, be aware of the fact that such a choice has far-reaching security implications. As a result, use this option with extreme caution. See "Accessing Shared Resources as Superuser" on page 16 for additional information.

Arguments that accept a client or host list (`ro=`, `rw=`, and `root=`) are guaranteed to work over the user datagram protocol (UDP), but may not work over other transport providers.

If you choose the `-d` option, the description is stored in the server's `sharetab` file. Clients will not see the description displayed when they use the `dfshares` command to list that server's shared resources.

The following set of examples illustrate the use of the `share` command.

The command:

```
share -F nfs /usr
```

shares the resource `/usr` with all of an issuing server's clients. Since no choice was specified, this resource is shared read/write by default.

To limit the client `yogi` read-only access to the resource `/usr`, enter

```
share -F nfs -o rw, ro=yogi /usr
```

As the `rw` option specifies, all other clients have read/write access.

To give the clients `bullwinkle` and `rocky` read/write access while limiting other clients to read-only access to `/usr`, enter

```
share -F nfs -o ro, rw=bullwinkle:rocky /usr
```

In the next example, the `-F NFS` option is omitted as the system is assumed to be NFS only. This lengthy command line is broken into several lines. A backslash (\) at the end of each line indicates that it is continued on the next line. The example illustrates the use of the `-d` option to describe the intent of a `share` command:

```
share -o ro, rw=bullwinkle:rocky \
-d "limit write access to rocky & bullwinkle" \
/usr
```

The `shareall` Command

The `shareall` command makes available a set of resources. To use the command, create a file that lists the resources you want to share. Each file entry consists of a single `share` command, each command having the syntax described in the previous section. That is, entries take the form

share [-F nfs] [-o *specific_options*] [-d *description*] [*pathname*]

Once this file is created, it becomes the input file to the `shareall` command. If no input file is specified, `shareall` uses the `/etc/dfs/dfstab` file by default.

If a hyphen (-) is entered in the place of specifying an input file, the system accepts standard input, allowing you to enter a number of `share` commands in succession. Once all desired commands have been entered, they can be executed all at once by pressing **Ctrl-D**. This is an alternative to entering one `share` command, waiting for the system to execute that command and return your prompt, then entering another command, and so on.

The `shareall` command has the form

```
shareall [-F nfs] [- | file]
```

where

`-F nfs`	indicates that resources should be shared over NFS; If NFS is the only file sharing package you have installed, you can omit the `-F nfs` option.
`-`	indicates that the command should accept standard input.
file	is the name of the file you created to be your input file.

To share the same set of resources on a fairly regular basis, without sharing them automatically, you can create an input file that contains a sequence of `share` commands. That file might looks like this:

```
#cat misc
share -F nfs -o ro,rw=art.dept /export/graphics
share -F nfs /usr/man
share -F nfs -o rw,ro=antelope,root=ocelot:rhino /local
```

Figure 2-1: Sharing Resources on a Regular Basis

To share the resources listed in the file `misc`, type

```
shareall misc
```

In this case, the `-F nfs` option is omitted from the `shareall` command, although it is included in the individual `share` commands in the input file. It might prove more convenient to change the command issued to

```
shareall -F nfs misc
```

In this case you can omit the individual references to NFS in each `share` command. If your system uses only NFS, the `-F` option can be omitted in both places.

The unshare Command

Resources that are shared either explicitly or automatically can be made unavailable for sharing at any time by means of the command `unshare`.

`unshare` is located in `/usr/sbin` and has the following syntax:

`unshare [ -F nfs ]` *pathname*

where

`-F nfs`	indicates that it is a resource to be unshared.
pathname	is the full name of the shared resource, beginning with root (/).

To stop sharing the directory `/usr`, enter the command

```
unshare -F nfs /usr
```

The `unshareall` Command

To stop sharing all the NFS resources currently shared on your system, use the `unshareall` command, located in `/usr/sbin`. If NFS is the only distributed file system installed on your system, enter

```
unshareall
```

If more than one distributed file system is installed, include the `-F nfs` option, as follows:

```
unshareall -F nfs
```

Automatic Sharing

Automatic sharing makes it easy to share the same set of resources on a regular basis. In the case of a server that supports diskless clients, automatic sharing makes the client machines' root directories available at all times.

Automatic sharing is controlled by the information found in the `dfstab` file, located in `/etc/dfs`. The `dfstab` file lists all the resources that a server is making available for sharing and controls which clients can access each of these resources. By editing the information in this file, resources can be added or deleted and the way sharing is done can be modified. The `dfstab` file can be modified with any text editor. The next time the machine enters run level 3, the system will read the updated `dfstab` file and use the information it contains to determine which resources are to be shared.

Each line in the `dfstab` file consists of a `share` command—the same command you might enter at the command line to share a resource explicitly. When used to share a resource over NFS, `share` has the following syntax:

`share [-F nfs] [-o` *specific-options*`] [-d` *description*`]` *pathname*

where

`-F nfs`	indicates that the resource is to be shared through NFS.
`-o` *specific-options*	is a comma-separated list of options that regulates how the resource is shared.
`-d` *description*	is a comment that describes the resource to be shared.
pathname	is the full name of the resource to be shared, starting at root (/).

If only one distributed file system package is installed, `nfs` is the default, and the `-F` option can be omitted.

The *specific options* that can follow the `-o` flag are the same as those available for the `share` command. See "The share Command" on page 9.

If the `-d` option is used, the *description* is stored in your `sharetab` file. It is not, however, displayed for clients when they use the `dfshares` command to list the resources shared on the system. `dfshares` is discussed in "Displaying Shared Local Resources" on page 25.

Accessing Shared Resources as Superuser

Under NFS, a server shares the resources it owns so that clients can mount them. Nevertheless, users who becomes the superuser at a client machine are denied access to mounted remote resources they would be able to see under their own UID. This restriction ensures that in becoming superuser, users do not gain access to files they would not ordinarily be able to see. When a user logged in as `root` requests access to a remote file shared through NFS, that UID is changed from `0` to that of the username `nobody` . User `nobody` has the same access rights as the public for a given file. For example, if the public has execute but not read or write permission for a file, then user `nobody` can only execute that file.

When sharing a resource, you can permit `root` on a particular machine to access to that resource by editing the file `/etc/dfs/dfstab` on the server, or by specifying the appropriate options at the command line.

For example, to allow the machine `samba`, but no other machine, superuser access to the shared directory `/usr/src`, enter the following command in the file `/etc/dfs/dfstab` or at the command line:

```
share -F nfs -o root=samba /usr/src
```

To allow more than one client root access, you must specify a list. Here, the machines `samba`, `mambo`, and `jazz` all are given root access to the directory `/usr/src`.

```
share -F nfs -o root=samba:mambo:jazz /usr/src
```

To give all client processes with UID `0`, that is. those logged in as `root` superuser access to `/usr/src`, enter

```
share -F nfs -o anon=0 /usr/src
```

`anon` is short for "anonymous." By default, anonymous requests inherit the UID of username `nobody`. NFS servers label as anonymous any request from a root user (someone whose current effective user UID is 0) not in the list following the `root=` option in the `share` command. The command shown above overrides the default behavior by telling the kernel to use the value 0 for anonymous requests. As a result, all root users retain their UID of 0.

For example, to allow users or processes on clients `sneezy` and `grumpy` with an effective UID of 0 to access `/usr` with superuser permission, enter

```
share -F nfs -o root=sneezy:grumpy /usr
```

To permit root access on `/usr` by any user or process whose user ID is 0, enter

```
share -F nfs -o anon=0 /usr
```

▼ ***Warning*** Resources should be shared in this way only if you are in a trusting environment.

❑ Mounting Resources

Once a resource has been shared on a server using NFS, that resource can be accessed from any client of that server, provided the client takes the steps necessary to mount the resource. Mounting can be done automatically when NFS operation begins on the client (when the client enters run level 3) or explicitly (by using the command line during a work session). If you regularly need to mount certain remote resources, it is best to set up automatic mounting when you first set up NFS operation.

Mounting and Unmounting Resources

An NFS shared resource can be explicitly mounted or unmounted at any time, using the `mount` and `umount` commands, respectively.

The `mount` Command

Clients can mount a remote resource, provided the resource is shared and located on a server that can be reached over the network. You must be superuser to use the `mount` command.

NFS supports two types of mounts—hard mounts and soft mounts. In the case of a hard mount, an NFS request affecting any part of the mounted resource is issued repeatedly until the request is satisfied. When a soft mount cannot be satisfied, an NFS request returns an error, then quits.

Before issuing the `mount` command, use the `mkdir` command to create a mount point for the remote resource. As with a local mount, if you mount a remote resource on an existing directory that contains files and sub-directories, the contents of the directory are obscured.

The `mount` command has the form

`mount [-F nfs] [-o` *specific-options*`]` *resource mountpoint*

where

`-F nfs` — is the type of mount to perform—in this case, an NFS mount. If the `-F` option is not specified, but *resource* or *mountpoint* is, `mount` looks in `/etc/vfstab` for the corresponding entry and mounts the resource according to the file system type specification there.

`-o` *specific-options* — is a list of options specific to NFS mounts. Some of the options are described below. The full set of options is described in "The Specific Options For share" on page 10.

resource — is in the form *server*`:`*pathname*, where *server* is the name of the machine sharing the resource and *pathname* is its location on the server.

mountpoint — is the pathname on the client through which users access the resource.

The Specific Options for `mount`

The *specific options* that can follow the `-o` flag are as follows:

`rw | ro` — indicates whether the mounting is to be done read-only or read/write. The default is `rw`.

`suid | nosuid` — indicates whether set-uid and set-gid bits are to be obeyed or ignored on execution, respectively. The default is `suid`.

`soft	hard`	indicates whether the resource should be mounted hard or soft. The default is `hard`.
`bg	fg`	indicates that `mount` should be retried in the background or in the foreground if the server does not respond. The default is `fg`.
`intr`	allows keyboard interrupts to kill a process that is hung while waiting for a response on a hard-mounted file system.
`retry=`*n*	is the number of times this `mount` should be retried.
`timeo=`*n*	sets the time-out to *n* tenths of a second. The default is 11.
`remount`	remounts a file system mounted read-only as read/-write.
`port=`*n*	sets the server's `IP` port number. The default is `NFS_PORT`.
`grpid`	creates a file with its group identifier (GID) set to the effective GID of the calling process. This behavior can be overridden on a per directory basis by setting the set-gid bit of the parent directory. In this case, the GID is set to the GID of the parent directory. Files created on resource systems that are not mounted with the `grpid` option obey BSD semantics; that is, the GID is unconditionally inherited from the parent directory.
`rsize=`*n*	sets the read buffer size to *n* bytes.
`wsize=`*n*	sets the write buffer size to *n* bytes.
`timeo=`*n*	sets the NFS time-out to *n* tenths of a second
`retrans=`*n*	sets the number of NFS retransmissions to *n*.
`secure`	calls for the use of the Secure NFS protocol described in "Using NFS" on page 7.
`noac`	suppresses attribute caching.
`acregmin=`*n*	holds cached attributes for at least *n* seconds after file modification.
`acregmax=`*n*	holds cached attributes for no more than *n* seconds after file modification.
`acdirmin=`*n*	holds cached attributes for at least *n* seconds after directory update.

`acdirmax=`*n*	holds cached attributes for no more than *n* seconds after directory update.
`actimeo=`*n*	sets *min* and *max* times for regular files and directories to *n* seconds.

Some Considerations When Using `mount`

Resources accessed through the `mount` command stay mounted during a work session, unless explicitly unmounted with the `umount` command. After exiting and re-entering run level 3, the resource will no longer be mounted (unless you edited the `vfstab` file to mount the resource automatically.)

When you mount an NFS resource:

- ▲ Consider soft mounting resources, so that client processes accessing the resources do not hang if the server goes down.
- ▲ Use the `hard` option with any resource you mount read/write. Then, if a user is writing to a file when the server goes down, the write continues when the server comes up again, and nothing will be lost.
- ▲ Use the `nosuid` option with any resource you mount read/write, unless you have good reasons to do otherwise.
- ▲ Use the `intr` option with any resource you mount `hard`, so that you can interrupt the current operation if the server goes down.

To soft mount on-line manual pages from remote machine `dancer` on the local directory `/usr/man` with the pages mounted read-only, type

```
mount -F nfs -o ro,soft dancer:/usr/man /usr/man
```

To hard mount the resource `/usr/local` from the remote machine `banjo` on the mountpoint `/usr/local/banjo`, with the resource mounted read/write, the set-uid bits ignored, and the keyboard interrupt enabled, enter the following, all on one line:

```
mount -F nfs -o hard,nosuid,intr \
banjo:/usr/local /usr/local/banjo
```

The `umount` Command

The `umount` command allows you to unmount a remote resource, whether the resource was mounted automatically or explicitly. You must be superuser to use `umount`. The `umount` command has the form:

`umount [` *resource* `|` *mountpoint* `]`

where

resource is the name of the server sharing the resource, followed by a colon and the pathname of the resource on the server.

mountpoint is the client directory where the remote resource is mounted.

Automatic Mounting

The file `/etc/vfstab` establishes which resources are mounted automatically.

A server can be the client of another server on a local network, in which case the server's `vfstab` may need to include both local and remote mounts.

Entries in the `/etc/vfstab` take the following form:

special fsckdev mountp fstype fsckpass automnt mntopts

where

special is the name of the server sharing the resource the client wants to mount, followed by a colon and the pathname of the resource to be mounted.

fsckdev is the name of a raw device; for a remote mount, the parameter is not applicable, and a hyphen (-) should be entered instead.

mountp is the mount point on the client through which the user accesses the resources mounted from the server.

fstype is the type of mount taking place. An NFS mount is indicated by `nfs`.

fsckpass is the pass number for multiple `fsck`'s. For a remote mount, the parameter is not applicable, and a hyphen (-) should be entered instead.

automnt indicates whether the entry should be mounted automatically (`yes`) or not (`no`) when the client enters run level 3.

mountopts is a list of comma-separated options identical to the options passed to `mount(1M)`.

The contents of `/etc/vfstab` remain the same until you change them.

To specify that the directory `/usr/local` on the server `dancer` should be mounted automatically on the client's directory `/usr/local/tmp` with read-only permission, add the following line to the client's `vfstab`.

```
dancer:/usr/local   -   /usr/local/tmp nfs - yes ro
```

❑ Obtaining Information

System administrators have at their disposal a variety of tools to obtain information about the status of the networked file system services. The commands described in this section allow you to determine what resources are available from remote servers, what resources your machine is making available for sharing or has mounted from remote file systems, and which of the shared resources made available by your machine have been mounted by remote clients.

Browsing Available Resources

The command `dfshares` allows you to "browse" remote servers to determine the names of remote resources available to your client machine. The syntax of the command is

```
dfshares [ -F nfs ] [ -h ] [ server ]
```

where

`-F nfs`	indicates that resources shared over NFS should be displayed.
`-h`	indicates that a header should not be printed in the display.
server	is a white space separated list of the name of servers whose shared resources should be displayed.

If NFS is the only file sharing package installed, omit the `-F nfs` option.

Unless it is suppressed with the `-h` option, the output from the `dfshares` command is preceded by the header

resource server access transport

where

resource	is of the form *server* : *pathname* .
server	is the name of the server sharing the resource.
access	is not currently used by NFS. A hyphen is used as a placeholder.
transport	is not currently used by NFS. A hyphen is used as a placeholder.

For example,

```
dfshares -F NFS birch - -
```

indicates a request for information regarding the NFS server birch. A header is printed as part of the display.

To obtain information on the servers coffee and tea, make the following request:

```
dfshares -F NFS coffee tea - -
```

Displaying Shared Local Resources

When given without arguments, the share command displays *all* the resources shared on your system, including the resources shared through NFS and those shared through other distributed files systems. It is not necessary to be superuser to use the share command for this purpose.

To list the remote resources currently available through NFS, enter

```
share
```

If more than one distributed file system package is installed on your system, the share command without arguments displays a list of *all* the shared resources on your system, including those shared through NFS.

Monitoring Shared Local Resources

The command dfmounts displays a list of shared resources by server. It lists the resources currently mounted over NFS, and by which clients. The command has the form

```
dfmounts [ -F nfs ] [ -h ] [ server ]*
```

where

`-F nfs`	indicates that resources mounted over NFS should be displayed.
`-h`	indicates that a header should not be printed in the display.
server	is the name of the server whose shared resources should be displayed.

If NFS is the only file sharing package you have installed, the `-F nfs` option can be omitted.

Unless it is suppressed with the `-h` option, the output from the `dfmounts` command is preceded by the header

resource server pathname clients

where

resource	is of the form *server:pathname*.
server	is the name of the server from which the resource was mounted.
pathname	is the pathname of the shared resource as it appears in the second part of *resource*.
clients	is a comma-separated list of clients that have mounted the resource.

The *server* can be any system on the network. If a *server* is not specified, `dfmounts` displays the resources of the local system that have been mounted by remote clients.

3

Handling NFS Problems

❑ Introduction

This chapter describes problems that can occur on machines using NFS services. The chapter includes

- ▲ An overview of the mount process.
- ▲ Strategies for tracking NFS problems.
- ▲ NFS-related error messages.

Before trying to clear NFS problems, you need some understanding of the issues involved. The information in this chapter contains sufficient technical details to give experienced network administrators an adequate picture of what is happening with their machines. It is not necessary to understand fully all the daemons, system calls, and files mentioned. However, you should be able to recognize their names and functions. Before you read this chapter, you should be familiar with the `mount` and `share` commands discussed previously and the daemons described in the next section.

❑ The NFS Daemons

NFS relies on a number of daemons. You should be aware of their existence and know how to restart them when necessary.

The `mountd` *Daemon*

`mountd` is an RPC server that answers file system mount requests. It reads the file `/etc/dfs/sharetab` to determine which file systems are available for mounting by which machines. It also provides information as to what file systems are mounted by which clients. This information can be obtained with the `dfmounts` command.

The `mountd` daemon is invoked automatically when your system enters run level 3.

The `mountd` command has the form

```
mountd [ -n ]
```

The `-n` option indicates that no check should be made to ensure that clients are root users. Using this option makes the system less secure, but is needed to allow compatibility with the pre-3.0 version of client NFS.

The `nfsd` *Daemon*

The `nfsd` daemons handle client file system requests. The `nfsd` command starts these daemons. It is automatically invoked when the system enters run level 3.

The `nfsd` command has the form

```
nfs [-a] [-p protocol] [-t device] [ nservers ]
```

where

`-a`	signifies that the `nfsd` daemons should be started over all available connectionless transports.
`-p` *protocol*	signifies that the `nfsd` daemons should be started over the specified protocol.
`-t` *device*	signifies that the `nfsd` daemons should be started for the transport specified by the given device.
nservers	is the number of file system request daemons to start. The value of *nservers* should be based on the load expected of the server. Four is the usual number.

The `biod` *Daemon*

The `biod` daemon is used on an NFS client to buffer read-ahead and write-behind. It starts a specified number of asynchronous block I/O daemons. The typical number is four.

The `biod` daemons are automatically invoked when the system enters run level 3.

The `biod` command has the form

```
biod [ nservers ]
```

where *nservers* is the number of servers to start.

❑ An Overview of the Mount Process

This section describes the remote mount process. As has been stated, NFS operation begins when your system enters run level 3.

1. The appropriate file in `/sbin/rc3.d` starts the `mountd` daemon and several `nfsd` daemons (the default is four). The `nfsd` daemons are used in server operation.
2. The same file in `/sbin/rc3.d` executes the `shareall` program, which reads the server's `/etc/dfs/dfstab` file, then tells the kernel which resources the server can share and what access restrictions, if any, are on these files.
3. The appropriate file in `/sbin/rc3.d` starts several (the default is four) `biod` daemons. The `biod` daemons are used in client operation.
4. The same file in `/sbin/rc3.d` starts the `mountall` program, which reads the client's `vfstab` file and mounts all NFS-type files mentioned there in a manner similar to an explicit mount, as described in the next section.

Mounting a Resource from the Command Line

The sequence of events that occur when a resource is mounted from the command line during a work session, is as follows:

1. The administrator enters a command, such as

   ```
   mount -F nfs -o ro, soft dancer:/usr/src \
   /usr/src/dancer.src
   ```

2. The `mount` command validates that the administrator has superuser permission, that the mount point is a full pathname, and that the file `/usr/lib/nfs/mount` exists. If all three of the conditions hold, `/sbin/mount` passes all the relevant arguments and options to `/usr/lib/nfs/mount`, which then takes control of the process. From this point forward, references to `mount` refer to this last file.
3. `mount` then opens `/etc/mnttab` and checks that the mount was not done automatically at the start of the work session.
4. `mount` parses the argument *special* into host `dancer` and remote directory `/usr/src`.
5. `mount` calls `dancer`'s `rpcbind` to get the port number of `dancer`'s `mountd`.
6. `mount` calls `dancer`'s `mountd` daemon and passes it `/usr/src`, requesting it to send a file handle `fhandle` for the directory.

7. The server's `mountd` daemon handles the client's mount requests. If the directory `/usr/src` is available to the client or to the public, the `mountd` daemon makes a `NFS_GETFH` system call on `/usr/src` to get the `fhandle`, which it sends to the client's mount process.
8. `mount` determines whether `/usr/src/dancer.src` is a directory.
9. `mount` makes a `mount (2)` system call with the `fhandle` and `/usr/src/dancer.src`.
10. The client kernel looks up the directory `/usr/src/dancer.src` and, if everything is in order, ties the file handle to the hierarchy in a mount record.
11. The client kernel looks up the directory `/usr/src` on `dancer`.
12. The client kernel does a `statfs (2)` call to `dancer`'s NFS server `nfsd`.
13. The `mount (2)` system call returns.
14. `mount` opens `/etc/mnttab` and adds an appropriate entry to the end, reflecting the new addition to the list of mounted files.
15. Once the resource is mounted, the client kernel sends the NFS RPC information to the server, where it is read by one of the `nfsd` daemons to process the file request.
16. The `nfsd` daemons know how a resource is shared from the information sent to the server's kernel by `share`. These daemons allow the client to access the resource according to its permissions.

❑ Determining Where NFS Service Has Failed

When tracking down an NFS problem, keep in mind that three main points of failure are possible: the server, the client, or the network itself. The strategy outlined in this section tries to isolate each of these components to find the one that is not working.

The `mountd` daemon must be present in the server for a remote mount to succeed. Make sure `mountd` is available for an RPC call by checking that `/sbin/init.d/nfs` has entries similar to those shown in Figure 3-1.

Figure 3-1: Checking **`mountd`** *Daemons*

```
if [ -x /usr/lib/nfs/mountd ]
then
        /usr/lib/nfs/mountd > /dev/console 2>&1
fi
```

Remote mounts also need a number of `nfsd` daemons to execute on NFS servers (the default is four). Check the server's file `/sbin/init.d/nfs` for lines similar to those shown in Figure 3-2.

Figure 3-2: Checking **`nfsd`** *Daemons*

```
if [ -x /usr/lib/nfs/nfsd ]
then
        /usr/lib/nfs/nfsd 4 > /dev/console 2>&1
fi
```

To enable these daemons without rebooting, become superuser and type

```
/usr/lib/nfs/nfsd 4
```

The client's `biod` daemons are not necessary for NFS to work, but they improve performance. Make sure the lines similar to those shown in Figure 3-3 are present in the client's file `/sbin/init.d/nfs`.

Figure 3-3: Checking **`biod`** *Daemons*

```
if [ -x /usr/lib/nfs/biod ]
then
        /usr/lib/nfs/biod 4 > /dev/console 2>&1
fi
```

To enable these daemons without rebooting, become superuser and type

```
/usr/lib/nfs/biod 4
```

Clearing Server Problems

When the network or server has problems, programs that access hard mounted remote files will fail in a different manner than those that access soft mounted remote files. Hard mounted remote resources cause the client's kernel to retry the requests until the server responds again. Soft mounted remote resources cause the client's system calls to return an error after trying for a while. `mount` is like any other program: if the server for a remote resource fails to respond and the `hard` option has been used, the kernel retries the mount until it succeeds. When `mount` is used with the `bg` option, it retries the mount in the background if the first mount attempt fails.

A program that tries to access a resource that is hard mounted hangs if the server fails to respond. In this case, NFS displays the message

`NFS server` *hostname* `not responding, still trying`

where *hostname* is the name of the unresponsive server. When the server finally responds, the message

`NFS server` *hostname* `ok`

appears on the console.

A program accessing a soft mounted resource whose server is not responding can choose to check the return conditions. If it does, it gets an error message of the form

. . .*hostname* `server not responding: RPC: Timed out`

If a client is having NFS trouble, check to ensure the server is up and running. From the client, type

`/usr/sbin/rpcinfo` *hostname*

to determine if the server is up. If the server is up and running, `rcpinfo` prints a list of program, version, protocol, and port numbers much like those shown in Figure 3-4.

***Figure 3-4:* *Sample* `rpcinfo`**

```
program   version   netid       address         service
 100000      3       icmp       0.0.0.0.0.111
 100000      2       icmp       0.0.0.0.0.111
 100000      3        udp       0.0.0.0.0.111
 100000      2        udp       0.0.0.0.0.111
 100000      3        tcp       0.0.0.0.0.111
 100000      2        tcp       0.0.0.0.0.111
 100000      3     ticotsord    sfrjn.rpc
 100000      3     ticots       sfrjn.rpc
 100000      3     ticlts       sfrjn.rpc
 100000      1        udp       0.0.0.0.4.8
 100000      1        tcp       0.0.0.0.4.133
```

If the server fails to print a list, try to log in at the server's console. If you can log in, check to make sure the server is running `rpcbind`.

If the server is up but your machine cannot communicate with it, check the network connections between your machine and the server.

Clearing Remote Mounting Problems

This section explains how to clear remote mounting problems. Any step in the remote mounting process can fail—some of them in more than one way. Below are the possible error messages and detailed descriptions of the failures associated with each. The `mount` command can get its parameters explicitly from the command line or from `/etc/vfstab`. The examples below assume command line arguments, but the same debugging techniques work if mounting is done automatically through `/etc/vfstab`.

- `mount: ... server not responding: RPC_PMAP_FAILURE - RPC_TIMED_OUT`

  The server sharing the resource you are trying to mount is down, is at the wrong run level, or its `rpcbind` is dead or hung. Check the server's run level by entering at the server the command shown below

  ```
  who -r
  ```

  If the server is at run level 3, try going to another run level and then back to run level 3, or try rebooting the server to restart `rpcbind`. Try to log in to the server from your machine, using the `rlogin` command. If you cannot log in, but the server is up, try to log in to another remote machine to check your network connection. If that connection is working, check the server's network connection.

- `mount: ... server not responding: RPC_PROG_NOT_REGISTERED`

  `mount` got through to `rpcbind`, but the NFS mount daemon `mountd` is not registered. Check the server's run level and make sure its daemons are running.

  ```
  mount: ...: No such file or directory
  ```

  Either the remote directory or the local directory does not exist. Check the spelling of the directory names. Use `ls` on both directories.

▲ `mount: not in share list for ...`

Your machine name is not in the list of clients allowed access to the resource you want to mount. From the client, you can display the server's share list by entering

```
dfshares -F nfs server
```

If the resource you want is not in the list, log in to the server and run the `share` command without options.

▲ `mount: ...: Permission denied`

This message indicates that you do not have the appropriate permissions or that some authentication failed on the server. You might not be in the share list (see the preceding error message and explanation) or the server might not believe you are who you say you are. Check the server's `/etc/dfs/sharetab` file.

▲ `mount: ...: Not a directory`

Either the remote path or the local path is not a directory. Check the spelling in your command and try to run `ls` on both directories.

The `mount` command hangs indefinitely if there are no `nfsd` daemons running on the NFS server. This happens when there is no `/etc/dfs/dfstab` file on the server when it enters run level 3. To clear the problem, restart the `nfsd` daemons by typing

```
/usr/lib/nfs/nfsd 4
```

❑ Fixing Hung Programs

If programs hang while doing file-related work, your NFS server may be dead. Under such circumstances, the following message might appear on your console:

```
NFS server hostname not responding, still trying
```

This message indicates that the NFS server *hostname* is down or that there is a problem with the server or network.

If your machine hangs completely, check the server or servers from which you mounted the resource. If one or more are down, do not be concerned. When the server comes back up, programs will resume automatically. No files will be destroyed.

If a resource is soft mounted and the server dies, other work should not be affected. Programs that time out trying to access soft mounted remote files fail with the message `errno ETIMEDOUT`. Other resources should still be accessible.

If all servers are running, determine if other users of these same servers are having trouble.

If more than one machine is having service problems, there is a problem with the server. Log in to the server. Run `ps` to see if `nfsd` is running and accumulating CPU time. Run `ps -ef` a few times, letting some time pass between each call. If no time is accumulating, you may be able to kill the daemons and then restart `nfsd`. If your attempt to kill the daemons and restart `nfsd` fails, you must reboot the server. If `nfsd` is not running, it may be that the server has been taken to a run level that does not support file sharing. Use `who -r` to obtain the server's current run level.

If other systems seem to be up and running, check your network connection and the connection of the server.

If programs on the client are hung but the server is up, NFS requests to the server other than reads and writes will succeed. If messages of the form

```
xdr_opaque: encode FAILED
```

are appearing on either the client or the server console, you may be requesting more data than the underlying transport provider can provide. Try remounting the file system using the `-o rsize=`*nnn*`,wsize=`*nnn* options to `mount (1M)` to restrict the request sizes the client will generate.

Fixing a Machine That Hangs During Booting

If your machine boots normally, then hangs when it tries to mount resources automatically, most likely one or more servers are down. Use `init` to go to single-user mode or to a run level that does not mount remote resources automatically. Then start the appropriate daemons in the background and use the `mount` command to mount each resource usually mounted automatically through the `/etc/vfstab` file. By mounting resources one at a time, you can determine which server is down. To restart a server that is down or hung, see the preceding section.

If you cannot mount any of your resources, it is likely that your network connection is bad.

Improving Access Time

If access to remote files seems unusually slow, type

```
ps -ef
```

on the server to be sure that it is not being affected adversely by a runaway daemon. If the display shows nothing unusual and other clients are getting good response, make sure the `biod` daemons are running. At the client, type

```
ps -ef | grep biod
```

Look for `biod` daemons in the display, then enter the command again. If the `biods` do not accumulate excessive CPU time, they are probably hung. If they are dead or hung, follow these steps:

1. Kill the daemon processes by typing

   `kill -9` *pid**

   where *pid* is the process identifier of a `biod` daemon you wish to kill.

2. Restart the `biod` daemons by typing

```
/usr/lib/nfs/biod 4
```

If the `biods` are running, check your network connection. The command `netstat -i` can help you determine if you are dropping packets.

4

The Automounter

❑ Introduction

Resources shared through NFS can be mounted or unmounted on an as-needed basis with the `automount` daemon. `automount` monitors all attempts to access directories associated with an automount map, along with any directories or files that reside under them. Whenever a user on a client machine running the automounter invokes a command that requires access to a remote file, the shared resource to which that file belongs is mounted automatically. After a specified amount of time elapses without that resource being accessed again, it is automatically unmounted.

With the automounter all mounting is done automatically and transparently as needed. It is unnecessary to set up mounting with the `vfstab` file or to use the `mount` and `umount` commands at the command line.

◆ ***Note*** Mounting some resources with `automount` does not exclude the possibility of mounting others with `mount`. In the case of a diskless machine you *must* mount root (/) and `/usr` with `mount`.

This chapter explains how the automounter works and provides instructions for setting it up and for dealing with problems that occur during its use.

❑ How the Automounter Works

Unlike mount, automount does not consult the file /etc/vfstab for a list of resources to mount. Rather, it consults a series of map files. All the information needed to mount the desired resources is maintained in the map files. The automounter consults the map file or files specified at the command line whenever the automount command is given.

The automounter mounts all requested resources under the directory /tmp_mnt. A symbolic link connects the requested mount point to the actual mount point. For example, when mounting the remote directory src under /usr, the automounter places the actual mount point in the directory /tmp_mnt/usr/src. The desired mount point, /usr/src, is a symbolic link to that location.

Figure 4-1: A Symbolic Link from the Requested to Actual Mount Point

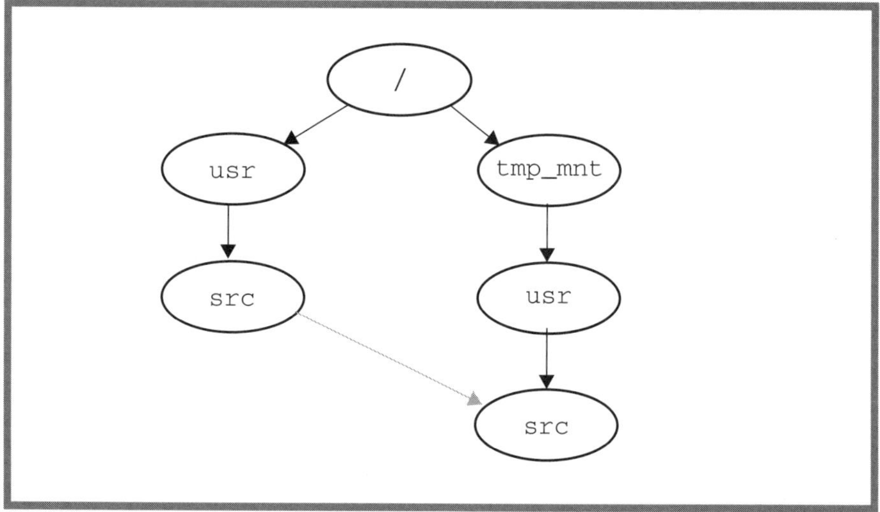

When automount is called, it forks a daemon to serve each mount point in the maps. Each daemon's job is to make the kernel believe that its mount has actually taken place. The daemon sleeps until a request is made to access the corresponding resource. At that point, the daemon intercepts the request, mounts the remote resource, creates a symbolic link between the requested mount point and the actual mount point under /tmp_mnt, passes the symbolic link to the kernel, and steps aside.

If a predetermined amount of time passes with the link untouched (typically five minutes), the daemon unmounts the resource and sleeps until its services are required once again.

A server neither knows nor cares whether the files it shares are accessed through `mount` or `automount`. As a result, no changes need be made to a server before the automounter is run from one of its client machines.

❑ Preparing the Maps

Automounter maps must reside in the `/etc` directory and can be created with any supported text editor.

There are three basic kinds of automounter maps: master maps, direct maps and indirect maps.

A master map contains the names of other maps which in turn contain the specific information needed to run the `automount` command.

A direct map contains all the information `automount` needs to do a mount. It can be called directly by the automounter or through a master map.

An indirect map mounts resources from several servers under a single mount point. Indirect maps can be called only through an entry in a master map as the master map specifies the mount point for the resources it lists.

Formatting Map Files

When creating automounter maps, you must follow these rules:

▲ Use a backslash before characters that might confuse the automounter's parser. For example, consider a directory whose name includes a colon, such as `rc0:dk1`. Without a backslash, this resource name might result in the map entry

```
/junk   -ro   vmsserver:rc0:dk1
```

The second colon will confuse the automounter. To avoid this problem, rewrite the entry as shown:

```
/junk -ro vmsserver:rc0\:dk1
```

- Use double quotes around a resource name if it includes white space.

```
/junk -ro "vms server":rc0
```

- Precede each line of a comment with the number sign (#). Use of a comment line in documenting a map entry is shown here:

```
#Mountpoint   Options        Location
/junk         -ro            vmsserver:rc0\:dk1
```

- To include a multi-line entry in a map, use backslashes to split the line into two or more shorter lines. For example, the entry

```
/usr/frame -ro,soft redwood:/usr/frame3.1 balsa:/export/frame
```

can be written as

```
/usr/frame -ro,soft  redwood:/usr/frame3.1 \
                     balsa:/export/frame
```

Creating a Master Map

Each line in a master map has the form:

mountpoint map [*mountoptions*]

where

mountpoint is the full pathname of the directory on which resources should be mounted. The *mountpoint* can be any designated directory.

map is the name of the map file that lists the resources to be mounted and their locations.

mountoptions is a comma-separated list of options that regulates the mounting of the entries mentioned in the map file. *mountoptions* can have any values that can be specified with the `mount` command, except for `fg` and `bg`. See Figure for further details.

◆ ***Note*** The mount options specified in the master map can be overridden by those contained in a given map entry.

A master map entry might read as follows:

```
/usr/man  /etc/libmap  -ro
```

This entry directs the automounter to mount everything listed in the indirect map `/etc/libmap` on `/usr/man` in the local file system. The `-ro` option specifies that the resource is to be mounted read-only. If, however, an entry in `libmap` indicates that a resource should be mounted read/write, that setting takes precedence.

If the master map calls a direct map, *mountpoint* is "`/-`". This designation tells the automounter to mount the entries in a direct map on the mount point specified in that map. (The *location* field in a direct map contains a full path-name).

A sample master map is shown in Figure 4-2.

```
#Mountpoint      Map                    Mountoptions
/usr/reports     /etc/reportmap         -rw,intr,secure
/usr/man         /etc/libmap            -ro
/-               /etc/direct.map        -ro,intr
```

Figure 4-2: Sample Master Map

This map has three entries. The first two contain indirect maps. The final entry, as the map name indicates, refers to a direct map and requires no mount point.

Creating a Direct Map

Entries in a direct map have the form

key [*mountoptions*] *location*

where

key	is the full pathname of the mount point.
mountoptions	is a comma-separated list of options that regulates the mounting of the resource specified in the entry.
location	is the location of the resource, specified as *server*:*pathname*.

Any of the options that can be specified with the `mount` command, except for `fg` and `bg`, can be specified as mount options. For a list of valid options, see See "The mount Command" on page 18.

A direct map entry might look as follows:

```
/usr/myfonts -ro,soft peach:/usr/fonts
```

This entry specifies that the remote resource `/usr/fonts` on the server `peach` should be soft mounted read-only on the local mount point `/usr/myfonts`. Whenever a user tries to access a file or directory that is part of the `/usr/fonts` directory tree, the automounter reads the direct map, mounts the resource from server `peach` onto the mount point `/tmp_mnt/usr/myfonts` on the local system, then creates a symbolic link between `/tmp_mnt/usr/myfonts` and `/usr/myfonts`. The user is unaware that the mount operation is taking place. From a user's point of view, the resource appears to be local and located at `/usr/myfonts`.

Figure 4-3 shows a typical direct map with three entries.

```
/usr/man              -ro,soft    oak:/usr/man \
                                  rose:/usr/man \
                                  willow:/usr/man
/var/spool/news       -ro,soft    pine:/var/spool/news
/usr/frame            -ro,soft    redwood:/usr/frame3.1 \
                                  balsa:/export/frame
```

Figure 4-3: Typical Direct Map

It is also possible to create map entries with more than one mount point and more than one location specified. For more information see Figure .

Creating an Indirect Map

Entries in an indirect map have the form

key [*mountoptions*] *location*

where

key	is the name of the directory that will be used as the mount point.
mountoptions	is a comma-separated list of options that regulates the mount.
location	is the location of the resource, specified as *server*:*pathname*.

In contrast to a direct map, the *key* is not the full path name of the directory to be used at the mount point.

In the case of an indirect map entry, the key is suffixed to its associated mount point. The association can be made from the command line or in the master map.

Consider the master map entry:

```
/usr/reports /etc/reportmap -rw,intr,secure
```

where `/etc/reportmap` is the name of the indirect map that lists the remote resources to be mounted under `/usr/reports`. This indirect map is shown in Figure 4-4.

Figure 4-4: Typical Indirect Map

```
#key           mountoptions       location
willow                            willow:/home/willow
cypress                           cypress:/home/cypress
poplar                            poplar:/home/poplar
pine                              pine:/export/pine
apple                             apple:/export/home
ivy                               ivy:/home/ivy
peach          -rw,nosuid         peach:/export/home
```

Assume this map resides on host `oak`. If user Leila has an entry in `oak`'s password database specifying her home directory as `/home/willow/leila`, whenever she logs into machine `oak`, the automounter will mount (as `/tmp_mnt/home/willow`) the directory `/home/willow` from machine `willow`. If one of the directories is indeed `leila`, Leila will be in her home directory.

Any option specified in the indirect map overrides all options specified in the master map or on the command line.

Specifying Multiple Mounts

An entry in a direct or indirect map can describe multiple mounts. Each of these mounts can be from different locations and can have different mount options. In the sample map below, the entry is split into three lines to improve its readability. That entry mounts `/usr/local/bin`, `/usr/local/share` and `/usr/local/src` from the server `ivy`, with the options `ro` (read-only) and `soft`.

```
/usr/local \
              /bin      -ro,soft   ivy:/export/local/sunsparc
              /share    -ro,soft   ivy:/export/local/share \
              /src      -ro,soft   ivy:/export/local/src\
```

Figure 4-5: Map Entry Describing Multiple Mounts

Another possible map entry is shown in Figure 4-6.

```
/usr/local \
      /bin      -ro,soft        ivy:/export/local/sun4 \
      /share    -rw,secure      willow:/usr/local/share \
      /src      -ro,intr        oak:/home/jones/src
```

Figure 4-6: Another Map Entry with Multiple Mounts

Here each directory is mounted with different options, and more than one server is used.

Multiple mounts can be hierarchical. When resources are mounted hierarchically, each resource is mounted on a subdirectory within another resource. When the root of the hierarchy is referenced, the automounter mounts the entire hierarchy. The concept of *root* here is very important. In the case of a single mount, there is no need to specify the root of the mount point, because it is assumed that the location of the mount point is at the mount root, or / . When mounting a hierarchy, however, the automounter must have a mount point for each mount within the hierarchy. The following illustration shows a true hierarchical mounting.

Figure 4-7: Map with Different Options and More than One Server

```
usr/local \
            /        -rw,intr     peach:/export/local \
            /bin     -ro,soft     ivy:/export/local/sun4 \
            /share   -rw,secure   willow:/usr/local/share \
            /src     -ro,intr     oak:/home/jones/src
```

The mount points used here for the hierarchy are `/`, `/usr/bin`, `/share`, and `src`. These mount point paths are relative to the *mount* root, not the host's *file system* root. The first entry in the example above has `/` as its mount point. It is mounted at the mount root. There is no requirement that the first mount of a hierarchy be at the mount root. The automounter issues `mkdir` commands to build a path to the first mount point if it is not at the mount root.

◆ *Note* A true hierarchical mount can be a problem if the server for the root of the hierarchy goes down. Any attempt to unmount the lower branches will fail, since the unmounting has to proceed through the mount root, which cannot be unmounted while its server is down.

Specifying Multiple Locations

A mount entry in a direct or indirect map can include more than one location in its *location* field. Mounting can be done from any of the locations specified.

Specifying multiple locations makes sense only when you are mounting a resource read-only, since you generally want to have control over the locations of files you write or modify. On-line documentation is an example of a read-only resource you might mount from a variety of locations. In a large network, the current set of on-line manual pages may be available from more than one server. It does not matter which server you mount them from, as long as that server is up and running and sharing its files. If manual pages reside in the directory `/usr/man` on three different hosts, called `oak`, `rose`, and `willow`, you can mount those manual pages from any location of those locations by specifying the following in the direct map:

```
/usr/man -ro,soft oak:/usr/man rose:/usr/man \
      willow:/usr/man
```

This could also be expressed as a comma-separated list of servers, followed by a colon and the pathname (as long as the pathname is the same on all servers):

```
/usr/man -ro,soft oak,rose,willow:/usr/man
```

From the list of servers, the automounter first selects those that are on the local network and queries or "pings" them. The first server to respond is selected, and an attempt is made to mount from it.

If the server goes down while the mount is in effect, the resource becomes unavailable. One option is to wait five minutes until the next autounmount takes place. At that point, the automounter chooses one of the available servers. Another option is to use the `umount` command, inform the automounter of the change in the mount table, and then retry the mount. See "Updating the Mount Table" on page 58." for more information.

Specifying Subdirectories

Until now the form *server*:*pathname* indicates a location in a map entry. You can also specify a subdirectory in the *location* field, using the syntax *server*:*pathname*:*directory*.

Assume a master map on host `oak` with the following entry:

```
/home   /etc/auto.home   -rw, intr, secure
```

Here `/etc/auto.home` is the name of an indirect map that contains the entries to be mounted under `/home`. The content of that map is as follows:

Figure 4-8: Specifying Subdirectory in Master Map

```
#key         mountoptions     location
cypress                       cypress:/home/cypress
poplar                        poplar:/home/poplar
pine                          pine:/export/pine
apple                         apple:/export/home
ivy                           ivy:/home/ivy
peach        -rw,nosuid       peach:/export/home
tessa                         willow:/home/willow:tessa
thea                          willow:/home/willow:thea
chloe                         willow:/home/willow:chloe
```

Consider the first entry in the map. Assume that user Sam has his home directory on host cypress and has an entry in host oak's password database specifying his home directory as /home/cypress/sam. If he logs in to oak, the automounter mounts (as /tmp_mnt/home/cypress) the directory /home/cypress residing on cypress. If one of the directories is sam, then Sam is in his home directory. Because of the options specified in oak's master map, Sam's home directory is mounted read/write, interruptible, and secure.

Next, consider the last three entries in the indirect map. These entries refer to the same resource on the same host (/home/willow). They also specify subdirectories in the *location* field (tessa, thea, and chloe).

When a user logs in to host oak and requests access to the home directory tessa on the host willow, the automounter mounts willow:/home/willow. It then places a symbolic link between /tmp_mnt/home/willow/tessa and /home/tessa.

If user Thea then tries to access her home directory from host oak, the automounter sees that willow:/home/willow is already mounted, so it simply returns the link between /tmp_mnt/home/willow/thea and the directory /home/thea.

In general, it is a good idea to provide a *subdirectory* entry in the *location* field when different map entries refer to the same resource shared by the same server.

Using Substitutions

If you have a map with a lot of subdirectories specified, as in the following indirect map, string substitutions can simplify map entries. Consider the following map:

```
#key          mountoptions     location
tessa                          willow:/home/willow:tessa
thea                           willow:/home/willow:thea
chloe                          willow:/home/willow:chloe
nancie                         pine:/export/home:nancie
emily                          peach:/export/home:emily
```

Figure 4-9: Using String Substitutions to Simplify Map Entries

The ampersand character (&) can be substituted for the key when it appears in the location field. After the substitution, the above map is simplified as follows:

```
#key          mountoptions     location
tessa                          willow:/home/willow:&
thea                           willow:/home/willow:&
chloe                          willow:/home/willow:&
nancie                         pine:/export/home:&
emily                          peach:/export/home:&
```

Figure 4-10: Substituting Ampersand for Key

If the server name is the same as the key as shown in the following example,

Figure 4-11: Server Name the Same as Key

```
#key        mountoptions    location
willow                      willow:/home/willow
peach                       peach:/home/peach
pine                        pine:/home/pine
oak                         oak:/home/oak
poplar                      poplar:/home/poplar
```

the use of the ampersand results in the simplification shown in Figure 4-12.

Figure 4-12: Specifying Subdirectory in Master Map

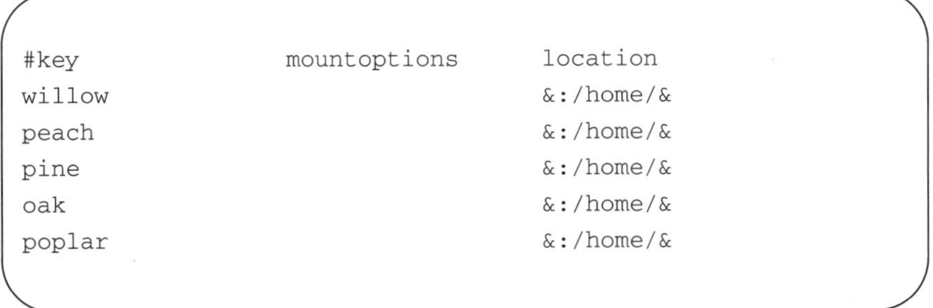

```
#key        mountoptions    location
willow                      &:/home/&
peach                       &:/home/&
pine                        &:/home/&
oak                         &:/home/&
poplar                      &:/home/&
```

If all entries in a map have the same format, you can use the catchall substitute character, the asterisk (*), as in Figure 4-13.

Figure 4-13: Using the Asterisk When All Map Entries Have the Same Format

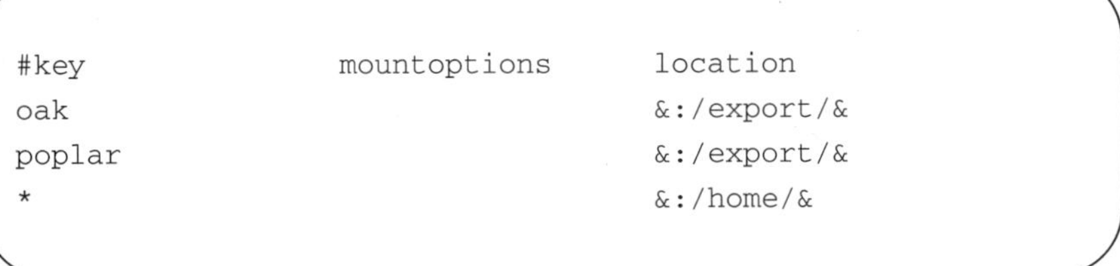

```
#key        mountoptions    location
oak                         &:/export/&
poplar                      &:/export/&
*                           &:/home/&
```

Once the automounter reads the catchall key, it does not continue to read the map.

Using Environment Variables

Use of environment variables can simplify the work of creating a map file. Such files can use variables inherited from the environment or those explicitly defined with the `-D` option on the command line. To use an environment variable in a map file, prefix a dollar sign (`$`) to its name. Braces can be used to separate the name of the variable from appended letters or digits.

If you want each client to mount the same client-specific files on several clients, create a specific map for each client. The line for host `oak` would be

```
/mystuff   cypress,ivy,balsa:/export/hostfiles/oak
```

That for `willow` will be

```
/mystuff   cypress,ivy,balsa:/export/hostfiles/willow
```

This scheme is viable on a small network, but maintaining this kind of host-specific map across a large network is not feasible. The solution is to define a variable `HOST` by invoking the automounter with a command line similar to the following:

```
automount -D HOST=`uname` ......
```

The direct map entry will be

```
/mystuff   cypress,ivy,balsa:/export/hostfiles/$HOST
```

Each host will find its own files in the `mystuff` directory, simplifying the task of centrally administering and distributing the maps.

❑ Invoking the Automounter

Once the maps are written, make sure that there are no equivalent entries in /etc/vfstab and that all the entries in the maps refer to NFS shared resources. At that point, the automounter can be invoked.

The automount command takes the following form:

```
automount [-mnTv] [-D name=vvalue ] [-f  master-file ] \
      [-M  mount-directory ] [-t  sub-options] \
      [directory  map  [-mountoptions] ] *
```

where

-m	Disable the search of the NIS map file.
-n	disables dynamic mounts. With this option, references through the automount daemon succeed only when the target file system has been previously mounted. This option can be used to prevent NFS servers from crossmounting each other.
-T	turns on trace to expand each NFS call and display it on standard output.
-v	turns on the verbose option to log status message to the console.
-D *name=value*	assigns a value to the indicated automount environment variable.
-M *mount-directory*	mounts temporary file systems in the named directory instead of in /tmp_mnt.
-t *suboptions*	specifies a command-separated list that contains any of the suboptions used with mount, with the exception of bg and fg, which may not be used. E.g., the suboptions are the same as those for NFS mount, with the exceptions noted.

The default mount point is `/tmp_mnt`. An alternate name can be chosen if the automount command is run with the `-M` option. For example,

```
automount -M /auto ...
```

places all mounts under the directory `/auto`.That directory is created by the automounter if it does not already exist.

The automounter can be invoked in any of the following ways:

▲ Specify all arguments without reference to the master map:

```
automount /net -hosts /home /etc/indirect_map \
-rw,intr,secure /- /etc/direct_map -ro,intr
```

▲ Specify all arguments in the master map and instruct the automounter to look in it for instructions:

```
automount -f /etc/master_map
```

▲ Specify mount points and maps in addition to those mentioned in the master map:

```
automount -f /etc/master_map /src \
/etc/auto.src -ro,soft
```

▲ Specify a master map while nullifying one of its entries. Nullifying one of the entries in the master map is particularly useful if you are using a map that you cannot modify but which does not meet the needs of your machine:

```
automount -f /usr/lib/master_map /home -null
```

▲ Specify a master map, but override one of its entries. Override an entry in the master map by specifying a different indirect map on the command line, as follows:

```
automount -f /usr/lib/master_map /home \
/myown/indirect_map -rw,intr
```

This command tells the automounter to mount /home according to instructions in /myown/*indirect_map*, not according to instructions in the indirect map specified in the master map.

❑ Modifying the Maps

Automounter maps can be modified at any time; however, the automounter looks at the master and indirect maps only when it is invoked. To force any changes to take effect, you must stop NFS operation and start it again by exiting and re-entering run level 3. This is unnecessary, however, in the case of a direct map. Changes to a direct map take effect the next time the automounter mounts the modified entry.

❑ Updating the Mount Table

If you use umount to unmount an automounted resource, you must direct the automounter to reread the /etc/mnttab file. This can be accomplished by sending signal 1 to the automount daemon, as shown below.

```
kill -1 pid
```

where *pid* is the automount process ID.

❑ Handling Automounter Problems

Should the automounter fail, you might see one of the following error messages:

- *mapname*: `Not found`

  The required map cannot be located. This message is produced only when the `-v` (verbose) option is given. Check the spelling and pathname of the map name.

- `dir` *mountpoint* `must start with '/'`

  The automounter mount point must be given as full pathname. Check the spelling and pathname of the mount point.

- *mountpoint*: `Not a directory`

  The *mountpoint* exists but is not a directory. Check the spelling and pathname of the mount point.

- `hierarchical mountpoint:` *mountpoint*

  The automounter does not allow itself to be mounted within an automounted directory. You need to think of another strategy.

- `WARNING:` *mountpoint* `not empty!`

  The mount point is not an empty directory. This message is produced only when the `-v` (verbose) option is given. It is a warning that the previous contents of *mountpoint* will no longer be accessible.

- `Can't mount` *mountpoint*: *reason*

  The automounter cannot mount itself at *mountpoint*. The stated reason should be self-explanatory.

- *hostname:filesystem* `already mounted on` *mountpoint*

  The automounter is attempting to mount a resource on a mount point, but the resource is already mounted on that mount point. This happens if an entry in `/etc/vfstab` is duplicated in an automounter map (either by accident or because the output of `mount -p` was redirected to `vfstab`). Delete one of the redundant entries.

- `WARNING:` *hostname:filesystem* `already mounted on` *mountpoint*

  The automounter is mounting itself on top of an existing mount point.

▲ `couldn't create` *directory*: *reason*

The system could not create a directory. The reason should be self-explanatory.

▲ `bad entry in map` *mapname "map entry"*

▲ `map` *mapname*, `key` *map key*: `bad`

The map entry is malformed, and the automounter cannot interpret it. Recheck the entry; perhaps some characters in it need escaping.

▲ *hostname*: `exports:` *rpc_err*

An error occurs when the automounter tries to get a share list from *hostname*. This indicates a server or network problem.

▲ `host` *hostname* `not responding`

▲ *hostname:filesystem* server `not responding`

▲ `Mount of` *hostname:filesystem* `on` *mountpoint*: *reason*

You will see these error messages after the automounter attempts to mount from *hostname* but gets no response or fails. This can indicate a server or network problem.

▲ *mountpoint -pathname* `from` *hostname*`: absolute symbolic link`

When mounting a resource, the automounter has detected that *mountpoint* is an absolute symbolic link (beginning with `/`). The content of the link is *pathname*. This circumstance can have undesired consequences on the client; for example, the content of the link may be `/usr`.

▲ `Cannot create socket for broadcast rpc:` *rpc_err*

▲ `Many_cast select problem:` *rpc_err*

▲ `Cannot send broadcast packet:` *rpc_err*

▲ `Cannot receive reply to many_cast:` *rpc_err*

All these error messages indicate problems attempting to "ping" servers for a replicated file system, possibly due to a network problem.

▲ `trymany: servers not responding:` *reason*

No server in a replicated list is responding. This situation may indicate a network problem.

▲ `Remount` *hostname:filesystem* `on` *mountpoint*: `server not responding`

An attempted remount after an unmount failed. This indicates a server problem.

▲ `NFS server (pid`*n@mountpoint*`) not responding still trying`

An NFS request made to the automount daemon with PID *n* serving *mountpoint* has timed out. The automounter might be temporarily overloaded or dead. Wait a few minutes. If the condition persists, the easiest solution is to reboot the client. If you do not want to reboot, exit all processes that make use of automounted resources (or, in the case of a shell, change to a non-automounted resource), kill the current automount process, and restart it again from the command line. If this procedure fails, you must reboot.

5

The sysadm Interface

❑ Introduction

The `sysadm` command invokes a visual interface that facilitates system administration. With the `sysadm` interface you can use a series of menus to set up and administer the NFS system.

The `sysadm` menu interface can be used to:

- ▲ Set up the NFS system.
- ▲ Start or stop the NFS system.
- ▲ Check to see if NFS is currently running.
- ▲ Manage local resources made available to other machines.
- ▲ Manage remote resources made available to your machine.

❑ Using sysadm

Invoked without arguments the `sysadm` command presents a series of menu options. It can also be invoked using the following syntax:

`sysadm [`*menuname* `|` *taskname*`]`

where

menuname	is the name of the desired menu.
taskname	is the name of the desired function.

If you invoke `sysadm` with a unique menu or task name, that command or task menu is immediately displayed. If the menu or task name specified is not unique, a menu of choices is displayed.

You can give the `sysadm` command a password, using the password task found in the `system_setup` menu. The same command can be used to change a password after it is set up.

Once a `sysadm` menu is accessed, help screens provide background information and explanations regarding menu selections. The Help function keysummons the help screens. The Cancel function key exits the help mode.

❑ Setting Up NFS

The `sysadm` setup procedure performs initial NFS setup on your machine. When the procedure is complete, everything necessary to run NFS on your system will have been done. This procedure assumes that the NFS software and the software utilities on which it depends are installed on your system. For information about installation, see "Installing NFS" on page 7.

To set up NFS by means of the `sysadm` interface, you invoke the interface and navigate through the menu options until you reach the proper setup menu, as in the following steps:

1. Log in as `root`.
2. At the UNIX prompt, type `sysadm network_services`. The main network services menu is displayed.
3. From the `network_services` menu, select the `remote_files` menu option.
4. From the `remote_files` menu, select `nfs_setup`.
5. From the `nfs_setup` menu, select `nfs`.

The screen shown in the following figure is now displayed.

```
Initial Network File System Setup

start   Start Network File System Operations
share   Share(s) Local Resources Automatically/Immediately
mount   Mount(s) Remote Resources Automatically/Immediately
```

Figure 5-1: NFS System Setup Screen

Execute each of the menu tasks in the order listed. Continue making interactive menu selections until the job is done. The Help function key provides additional information as requested.

❑ Starting and Stopping NFS

This `sysadm` procedure starts and stops NFS. It will determine if NFS is running.

1. Type `sysadm network_services`.
2. From the `network_services` menu, select `remote_files`.
3. From the `remote_files` menu, select `specific_ops`.
4. From the `specific_ops` menu, select `nfs`.
5. From the `nfs` menu, select `control`.

The screen shown in the following figure is now displayed.

Figure 5-2: NFS System Control Screen

```
The Network File System Control

check_status     Check Status of NFS File Service
start            Start Network File System Operations
stop             Stop Network File System Operations
```

- ▲ To determine whether NFS file service is running, select `check_status`.
- ▲ To start the NFS system, select `start`.
- ▲ To stop the NFS system, select `stop`.

❑ Local Resource Sharing

The local resource sharing procedure allows you to make local resources available or unavailable (share/unshare) to remote systems via NFS. With this `sysadm` interface, you can choose either to have this happen automatically when NFS is started or when needed during a work session. You can also modify the options by which local resources are shared. Finally, the procedure allows you to list the local resources that are currently shared via NFS.

To set up local resource sharing:

1. Type `sysadm network_services`.
2. From the `network_services` menu, select `remote_files`.
3. From the `remote_files` menu, select `local_resources`.

The screen shown in the following figure is now displayed.

```
Local Resource Sharing Management

list     List Automatically/Currently Shared Local Resources
modify   Modify Automatic/Current Sharing of Local Resources
share    Share Local Resources Automatically/Immediately
unshare  Stop Automatic/Current Sharing of Local Resources
```

Figure 5-3: Local Resource Sharing Management Screen

- To list the local resources currently shared by NFS, select `list`, then `nfs`.
- To modify sharing permissions of local resources via NFS, select `modify`, then `nfs`.
- To share local resources via NFS, select `share`, then `nfs`.
- To unshare local resources currently shared via NFS, select `unshare`, then `nfs`.

See the sections "Sharing and Unsharing Resources" on page 8, "Mounting Resources" on page 17 and "Obtaining Information" on page 23 for more information about these tasks.

❑ Remote Resource Mounting

Use the `sysadm` procedure to make remote resources available or unavailable (mount/unmount) to your local computer via NFS. With it, you can specify resources to be mounted or unmounted automatically, whenever NFS operation stops and starts. Alternatively, you can mount and unmount a resource immediately during a work session or you can modify the options by which remote resources are mounted on your local computer. Finally, this procedure enables you to list the remote resources currently available to your machine.

1. Type `sysadm network_services`.
2. From the `network_services` menu, select `remote_files`.
3. From the `remote_files` menu, select `remote_resources`.

You are now at the following screen.

Figure 5-4: Remote Resource Access Management

```
Remote Resource Access Management

list     List Automatically/Currently Mounted Remote Resources
modify   Modify Automatic/Current Mounting of Remote Resources
mount    Mount Remote Resources Automatically/Immediately
unmount  Stop Automatic/Current Mounting of Remote Resources
```

- ▲ To list remote resources mounted via NFS, select `list`, then `nfs`.
- ▲ To modify mount permissions of remote resources, select `modify` then `nfs`.
- ▲ To mount remote resources, select `mount`, then `nfs`.
- ▲ To terminate mounting of remote resources currently shared via NFS, select `unmount`, then `nfs`.

For additional information on these tasks, see the section "Sharing and Mounting Resources Explicitly" and "Obtaining Information" for details.

6

Secure NFS

❑ Introduction

NFS is a powerful and convenient way to share resources on a network with different machine architectures and operating systems. However, the same features that make sharing resources through NFS convenient also pose some security problems.

An NFS server authenticates a file request by authenticating the machine, not the user, making the request. If the superuser privilege is not restricted when a resource is shared, a client user could run the `su` command and impersonate the owner of a file. For additional information, see "Accessing Shared Resources as Superuser" on page 16.

Given root access and a good knowledge of network programming, it is possible to inject arbitrary data into the network and to pick up any data from the network.

The most dangerous attacks involve the injection of data. This might mean impersonating a user by generating the right packets or by recording "conversations" and replaying them later. Such attacks affect data integrity. Attacks involving passive eavesdropping—merely listening to network traffic without impersonation—are not as dangerous, since data integrity is not compromised. Encryption can be used to protect the sensitive information that goes over the network.

A common approach to network security problems is to leave the solution to each application. A better approach is to implement a standard authentication system at a level that covers all applications. This is the approach taken by Secure NFS.

System V Release 4.0 includes an authentication system at the level of the Remote Procedure Call (RPC). RPCs are the mechanism on which NFS is built. This system, known as Secure RPC, greatly improves the security of network environments and provides additional security to NFS. The security features it provides to NFS are known as Secure NFS.

Because Secure RPC is at the core of Secure NFS, it is necessary to understand how authentication works in RPC. This chapter

- Provides an overview of Secure RPC.
- Explains how to set up Secure NFS.
- Presents points to be aware of if you plan to use Secure NFS.

❑ An Overview of Secure RPC

Secure RPC is designed to build a system at least as secure as a time-shared system. In a time-sharing system users are authenticated through a login password. Users can log in on any remote machine, just as they can on a local terminal. Their login passwords control their network access. In time-sharing, the trusted person is the system administrator, who has an ethical obligation not to change a password in order to impersonate someone. In secure RPC, the network administrator is trusted not to alter entries in a database that stores "public keys."

The RPC authentication system relies on two key concepts: *credentials* and *verifiers.* For example, an ID badge containing identifying information— a name, address, birth date, and so on—might serve as a credential; the photo attached to the badge is a verifier. To ensure that the badge is not stolen, you can check the photo on the badge against the person carrying it. Client processes send both a credential and a verifier to the server with each RPC request. The server sends back only a verifier, since clients know the server's credentials.

RPC's authentication is open-ended, allowing a variety of authentication systems to be plugged into it. Currently, there are two such systems: UNIX system and Data Encryption Standard (DES).

When a network service uses UNIX system authentication, the credentials contain the client's machine name, user identification number (UID), group identification number (GID), and group access list. The verifier contains nothing. Because there is no verifier, a root user could deduce appropriate credentials, using commands such as `su`. UNIX system authentication also assumes that all machines on a network are UNIX system machines. As a result, it breaks down when applied to other operating systems in a heterogeneous network.

To overcome the problems inherent in UNIX system authentication, Secure RPC uses DES authentication—a scheme that employs verifiers, yet allows Secure RPC to be general enough to be used by most operating systems.

DES Authentication

DES authentication uses the Data Encryption Standard (DES) and public key cryptography to authenticate both users and machines in a network. DES is a standard encryption mechanism. Public key cryptography is a cipher system that involves two keys: one public and one secret.

DES authentication relies on a sender's ability to encrypt the current time. The receiver decrypts that time and checks it against its own clock. Two things are necessary for this scheme to work:

- The two agents must agree on the current time.
- The sender and receiver must be using the same encryption key.

If a network runs a time-synchronization program, the time on the client is automatically synchronized with that of the server. If a time-synchronization program is not available, timestamps are computed, using the server's time instead of the network time. In this case, the client asks the server for the time before starting the RPC session, then computes the time difference between its own clock and the server's. This difference is used to offset the client's clock when computing timestamps. If the client and server clocks become synchronized to the point where the server begins to reject the client's requests, the DES authentication system resynchronizes with the server.

The client and server arrive at the same encryption key by generating a random *conversation key.* They then use public key cryptography to deduce a *common key.* The common key is one that only the client and server are capable of deducing. The conversation key is used to encrypt and decrypt the client's timestamp. The common key is used to encrypt and decrypt the conversation key.

A Secure RPC Client/Server Session

The following series of transactions takes place in a client/server session using Secure RPC.

Step 1 Sometime prior to a transaction, the user runs a program that generates a *public key* and a *secret key.* (Each user has a unique public key and a unique secret key.) The public key is stored, in encrypted form, in a public database. The secret key is stored, also in encrypted form, in a private directory.

Step 2

a. The user logs in and runs the `keylogin` program. Alternatively, the `keylogin` program can be included in `/etc/profile`, in which case it runs automatically whenever the user logs in.

b. The `keylogin` program prompts the user for a secure RPC password, which is then used to decrypt the secret key.

c. The `keylogin` program passes the decrypted secret key to the Keyserver, an RPC service with a local instance on every machine.

d. The Keyserver saves the decrypted secret key and waits for the user to initiate a transaction with a server.

Step 3 When the user initiates a transaction with a server,

a. The Keyserver randomly generates a *conversation key.*

b. The kernel uses the conversation key to encrypt, among other things, the client's timestamp.

c. The Keyserver looks up the server's public key in the public database.

d. The Keyserver uses the client's secret key and the server's public key to create a *common key.*

e. The Keyserver encrypts the conversation key with the common key.

Step 4 The transmission, including the timestamp and the conversation key, is sent to the server. The transmission includes a credential and a verifier. The credential contains

- The client's machine name.
- The conversation key, encrypted by means of the common key.
- A "window," encrypted with the conversation key.

  The window is the difference the client says should be allowed between the server's clock and the client's timestamp. If the difference between the server's clock and the timestamp is greater than the window, the server should reject the client's request. For secure NFS, the window defaults to 30 minutes.

The client's verifier contains

- The encrypted timestamp.
- An encrypted verifier of the specified window, incremented by 1.

  The window verifier minimizes the chance that a randomly chosen credential will be successful just by chance; for example an unauthorized user might write a program that fills the fields of the credential and verifier with random bits. The server then decrypts the conversation key into some random key. That key is then used to try to decrypt the window and the timestamp. The result is random but after a few thousand trials there is a good chance that the random window/timestamp pair will pass the authentication system. The window verifier makes guessing the right credential much more difficult.

Step 5 When the server receives the transmission from the client,

a. The Keyserver local to the server looks up the client's public key in the public database.

b. The Keyserver uses the client's public key and the server's secret key to deduce the common key—the same common key computed by the client. No one but the server and the client can calculate the common key, because doing so requires knowing one secret key or the other.

c. The kernel uses the common key to decrypt the conversation key.

d. The kernel calls the Keyserver to decrypt the client's timestamp with the decrypted conversation key.

Step 6 After the server decrypts the client's timestamp, it stores four things in a credential table:

- The client's machine name.
- The conversation key.
- The window.
- The client's timestamp.

The first three things are stored for future use. The timestamp is stored to protect against replays. The server accepts only timestamps that are chronologically greater than the last one seen, so any replayed transactions are guaranteed to be rejected.

Step 7 The server returns a verifier to the client, which includes

- The index ID, which the server records in its credential table.
- The client's timestamp minus one, encrypted by conversation key.

One is subtracted from the timestamp is to insure that it is invalid and cannot be reused as a client verifier.

Step 8 The client receives the verifier and authenticates the server. The client knows that only the server could have sent the verifier, because only the server knows what timestamp the client sent.

Step 9 The client returns the index ID to the server in its second transaction and sends another encrypted timestamp.

Step 10 The server sends back the client's timestamp minus 1, encrypted by the conversation key.

With every transaction after the first, the client sends its index ID and another encrypted timestamp. The server returns the timestamp minus 1.

 ***Note*** The name of caller must be authenticated in some manner. The Keyserver cannot use DES authentication to do this, since it would create a deadlock. The Keyserver solves this problem by storing the secret keys by UID and only granting requests to local root processes. The client process then executes a setuid process, owned by root, which makes the request on the part of the client, telling the Keyserver the real UID of the client.

❑ Administering Secure NFS

To use Secure NFS, machines must have a domain name. A *domain* is an administrative entity, typically consisting of several machines, that joins a larger network. If you are running NIS, you should also establish the NIS name service for the domain.

With UNIX system authentication, the name of a domain is the UID. UIDs are assigned per domain. A problem with this scheme is that UIDs clash when domains are linked across the network. Another problem has to do with superusers. With UNIX system authentication, the superuser ID (UID 0) is assigned one per machine, not one per domain. This means that a domain can have multiple superusers—all with the same UID.

DES authentication corrects these problems by using netnames. A *netname* is a string of printable characters created by concatenating the name of the operating system, a user ID, and a domain name. For example, a UNIX system user with a user ID of 508 in the domain `eng.acme.COM` would be assigned the netname: `unix.508@eng.acme.COM`. Because user IDs are unique within a domain and because domain names are unique on a network, this scheme produces a unique netname for every user.

To overcome the problem of multiple superusers per domain, netnames are assigned to machines as well as to users. A machine's netname is formed much like a user's—by concatenating the name of the operating system and the machine name with the domain name. A UNIX system machine with the name `hal` in the domain `eng.acme.COM` would have the netname `unix.hal@eng.acme.COM`.

In summary, take the following sequence of steps when setting up a secure NFS machine.

1. Assign a domain name and make that name known to each machine in the domain. A domain name is the concatenation of all the labels of the domain from the root to the current domain, listed from right to left and separated by periods.
2. Establish public keys and secret keys for clients' users by means of the `newkey` command or have users establish their own public and secret keys with the `chkey` command.

   When public and secret keys have been generated, the public keys are stored in the `publickey` database, and users' secret keys are stored in `/etc/keystore`. Secret keys for root users are stored in `/etc/.rootkey`.
3. If the `keylogin` program is in `/etc/profile`, it will run automatically whenever a user logs in. Otherwise, users must run `keylogin` when they log in.
4. If you are running YP, verify that the `ypbind` daemon is running and that `ypserv` is running in the domain.
5. Verify that the `keyserv` daemon (the Keyserver) is running by typing

   ```
   ps -ef | grep keyserv
   ```

   If the Keyserver is not running, start it by typing

   ```
   /usr/sbin/keyserv
   ```

6. Edit the `/etc/dfs/dfstab` file and add the `secure` option to the appropriate entries (those that indicate resources you want clients to mount using DES authentication).
7. On each client machine, edit `/etc/vfstab` to include `secure` as a mount option in the appropriate entries (those that indicate resources that should be mounted using DES authentication).

◆ ***Note*** If a client does not mount as `secure` a resource that is shared as secure, everything works, but users have access as user `nobody`, rather than as themselves.

If NIS is not running, users must keep their secret keys synchronized with their login passwords. If they change their entries in the password database, they must invoke `chkey`.

When reinstalling, moving, or upgrading a machine, it is necessary to save `/etc/keystore` and `/etc/.rootkey`.

Creating and Changing Keys

The `newkey (1M)` command is used to create a new key in the public key database. The `newkey` command is run by a network administrator on the machine containing the `publickey(4)` database to establish public keys for users and privileged users on the network. newkey prompts for a password for the given username or hostname and then creates a new public/secret key pair for the user or host in `/etc/publickey`, encrypted with the given password. Its syntax is

```
newkey -h hostname | newkey -u username
```

where

`-h` *hostname*	creates a new public/secret key pair for the privileged user at *hostname* and then prompts for a password for *hostname*.
`-u` *username*	creates a new public/secret key pair for the given user name and then prompts for the given user name.

The `chkey` command is the change-user encryption key. It prompts for a password and uses that password to encrypt a new user encryption key. The new key is then stored in the `publickey(4)` database. This command can only be executed on the master server for that database.

The command has the syntax

```
chkey
```

❑ Important Considerations

You should be aware of the following points if you plan to use Secure NFS:

- When a server crashes, all of the secret keys that are stored on the system are lost. At this point, no process is able to access secure network services or to mount an NFS file system. The important processes at this time are usually root processes. Things would work if root's secret key were stored away, but if no one is present at the time of the crash, such as might be the case after a power failure, nobody will be around to type the password that decrypts the root's secret key. If the machine has a local disk, the solution to the problem is to store root's decrypted secret key in a file that the Keyserver can read.
- Some systems boot in single-user mode, with a root login shell on the console and no password prompt. Physical security is imperative in such cases.
- Booting a diskless client machine is not totally secure. It is possible for someone to impersonate the boot-server and boot a devious kernel, for example, one that makes a record of your secret key on a remote machine. Secure NFS provides protection only after the kernel and the Keyserver are running. Before that, there is no way to authenticate the replies given by the boot-server. This situation is not considered a serious problem, because it is highly unlikely that somebody would be able to write this compromised kernel without source code. Also, the crime is not without evidence. If you poll the network for boot-servers, you will discover the devious boot-server's location.
- Most setuid programs are owned by root. Since root's secret key is always stored at boot time, these programs will behave as they always have. If a setuid program is owned by a user, however, it may not work. For example, if a setuid program is owned by `dave`, and `dave` has not logged into the machine since it booted, the program would not be able to access secure network services.
- If you use `keylogin` to gain access to a remote machine (using `login`, `rlogin`, or `telnet`), you give away access to your account: your secret key gets passed to that machine's Keyserver, which then stores it. This is only a concern if you do not trust the remote machine. If you have doubts, do not log in to a remote machine that requires a password. Instead, use NFS to mount resources shared by the remote machine. As an alternative, you can use `keylogout`(1) to delete the Keyserver.

- ▲ Using secure NFS can result in some degradation of network performance. Not all file operations go over the network, so the impact on total system performance is not too great. Secure NFS is an optional feature. Environments that require higher performance at the expense of security can turn it off.

7

The Network Lock Manager

❑ Introduction

Locking prevents multiple processes from modifying the same file at the same time and allows cooperating processes to synchronize access to shared files. NFS uses the network locking facility implemented with the user-level daemon, the Network Lock Manager [`lockd(1m)`].

The lock manager supports the UNIX System V style of advisory and mandatory file and record locking. Users communicate with the network locking service via the standard `fcntl()` system-call interface. User calls to the `fcntl()` system call or to the `lockf()` library call are mapped to RPC-based messages to the local lock manager. The fact that the file system may be spread across multiple machines is not a complication—until a crash occurs.

In an NFS environment, where multiple machines can access the same file at the same time, the process of recovering from a crash is more complex than in a non-network environment. Locking is inherently stateful. It requires that the server maintain client information from one transaction to the next. If a server crashes, clients holding locks on server files must be able to recover their locks when the server recovers. If a client crashes, its servers must release the locks held by processes running on the client. Additionally, to preserve NFS transparency, the recovery of lost locks must not require the intervention of applications.

Basic file access operations, such as read and write, use the stateless NFS protocol. All interactions between NFS servers and clients are atomic—the server does not remember anything about its clients from one interaction to the next. In the case of a server crash, client applications sleep until the server comes back up and their NFS operations can complete.

Stateful services, such as the locking service, are not part of NFS per se. They are separate services that use the status monitor to ensure that their implicit network state information remains consistent with the real state of the network. Two specific state-related problems are involved in providing locking in a network context:

- If the client crashes, its locks can be held forever by the server.
- A server that crashes loses its state, including all its lock information, when it recovers.

The Network Lock Manager solves both of these problems by cooperating with the Network Status Monitor to ensure that it is notified of relevant machine crashes. Its own protocol then allows it to recover the lock information it needs when crashed machines recover.

The Network Lock Manager and the Network Status Monitor [`statd (1M)`] are user-level network-service daemons. They are essential to the kernel's ability to provide fundamental network services and are run on all network machines. Like other network-service daemons, they are best seen as extensions to the kernel, which, for reasons of space, efficiency, and organization, are implemented as daemons.

Application programs that need a network service can call the appropriate daemon directly with RPC/XDR or use a system call. In the latter case, the kernel uses RPC to call the daemon. The network daemons communicate among themselves with RPC. (See "The Locking Protocol" on page 84 for details regarding the lock manager protocol.)

The daemon-based approach to network services allows for tailoring by users needing customized services. For example, users can alter the lock manager to provide a different style of locking.

Figure 7-1 depicts the architecture of the locking service.

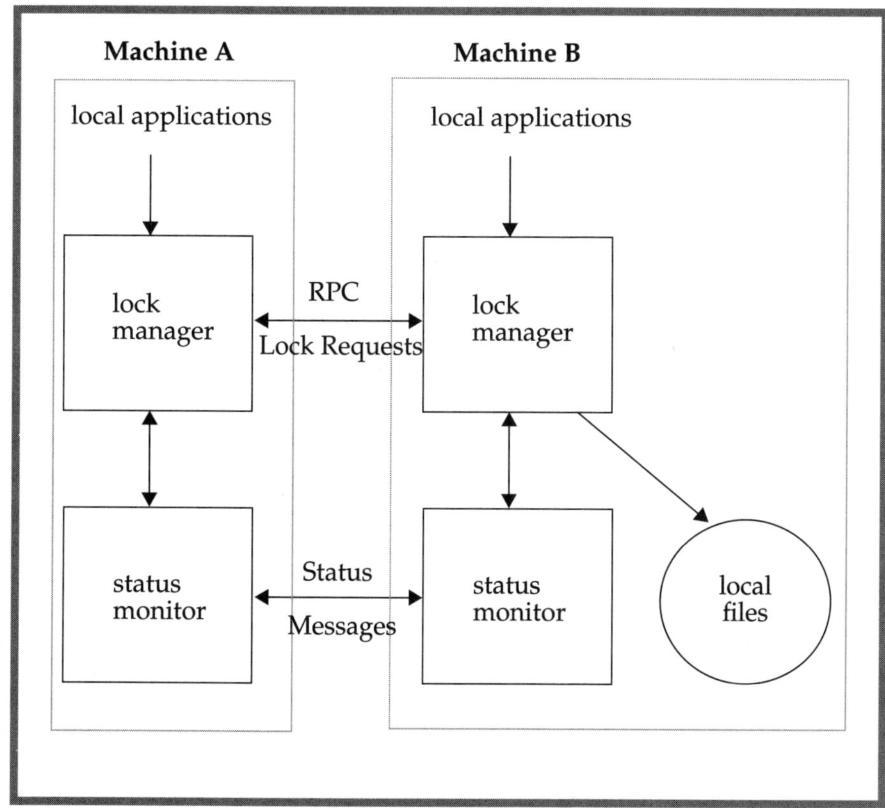

Figure 7-1: Locking Service Architecture

At each server site, a lock manager process accepts lock requests, made on behalf of client processes by a remote lock manager or on behalf of local processes by the kernel. The client and server lock managers communicate by means of RPC calls. Upon receiving a remote lock request for a machine that it does not already hold a lock on, the lock manager registers its interest in that machine with the local status monitor and waits for that monitor to notify it that the machine is up. The monitor continues to watch the status of registered machines and notifies the lock manager if one of them is rebooted after a crash. If the lock request is for a local file, the lock manager tries to satisfy it and communicates back to the application along with the appropriate RPC path.

The crash recovery procedure is very simple. If a client failure is detected, the server releases the failed client's locks, on the assumption that the client application will request locks again as needed. If the recovery (and, by implication, the crash) of a server is detected, the client lock manger retransmits all the lock requests previously granted by the recovered server. The retransmitted information is used by the server to reconstruct its locking state.

The locking service is essentially stateless. More precisely, its state information is carefully circumscribed within a pair of system daemons that handle automatic, application-transparent crash recovery. If a server crashes and loses its state, it expects that its clients will be notified of the crash and that they will send it the information it needs to reconstruct its state. The key to this approach is the status monitor, which the lock manager uses to detect both client and server failures.

`lockd [1m]` has the syntax

`/usr/lib/nfs/lockd [-t` *timeout*`] [-g` *graceperiod*`]`

where

`-t` *timeout*	specifies the seconds to wait before retransmitting a lock request to a remote server. The default value is 15.
`-g` *graceperiod*	is the number of seconds a recovered server waits for all client-site lock daemons to resubmit lock requests. The default value is 45.

❑ The Locking Protocol

The lock manager processes lock requests sent locally by the kernel or remotely by another lock daemon. There are four basic kernel-to-lock manager requests:

`KLM_LOCK`	Lock the specified record.
`KLM_UNLOCK`	Unlock the specified record.
`KLM_TEST`	Determine if the specified record is locked.
`KLM_CANCEL`	Cancel an outstanding lock request.

The lock manager forwards remote lock requests to a server's lock daemon by means of RPC/XDR. Once the request is sent, the lock manager asks that the status monitor begin its work. This request waits until the server's `lock` and `statd` daemons have replied.

Despite the fact that the Network Lock Manager adheres to the `lockf()` and `fcntl()` semantics, a few subtle points about its behavior deserve mention. These arise directly from the nature of the network.

- ▲ When an NFS client goes down, the lock managers on all of its servers are notified of the crash by their status monitors. They release that client's locks, on the assumption that it will request them again when it wants them. When a server crashes, however, matters are different. Clients will wait for the server to come back up. When it does, the server's lock manager gives the client lock managers a grace period in which to submit lock reclaim requests. During this period, the server accepts only reclaim requests. The client's status monitors notify their respective lock managers when the server recovers. The default grace period is 45 seconds.
- ▲ It is possible that, after a server crash, a client will not be able to recover a lock it had on a file on that server. This will happen if another process has claimed the lock before the recovering application process can do so. In this case the SIGLOST signal is sent to the process. By default, this signal kills the application.
- ▲ The local lock manager does not reply to a kernel lock request until the server lock manager responds. Further, if the lock request is on a server new to the local lock manager, the lock manager registers its interest in that server with the local status monitor and waits for its reply. Thus, if either the status monitor or the server's lock manager is unavailable, the reply to a lock request for remote data is delayed until both the status monitor and the server's lock manager become available.

❑ The Network Status Monitor

The lock manager relies on the Network Status Monitor to maintain the inherently stateful locking service within the stateless NFS environment. The status monitor, implemented as `statd(1M)`, is very general and can also be used to support other stateful network services and applications. Crash recovery typically is one of the most difficult aspects of network application development, requiring a major design and installation effort. The status monitor makes crash recovery more or less routine.

The status monitor provides a general framework for collecting network status information. Implemented as a daemon that runs on all network machines, the status monitor provides a simple protocol that allows applications to monitor easily the status of other machines. Its use improves overall robustness and avoids situations in which applications running on different machines (or even on the same machine) come to disagree about the status of a site—a potentially dangerous situation that can lead to inconsistencies in many applications.

Applications use the status monitor by registering with it the machines that they are interested in. The monitor then tracks the status of those machines and, when one of them crashes (actually, when one of them recovers from a crash), it notifies the interested applications. The applications take whatever actions are necessary to reestablish a consistent state. This approach provides the following advantages:

- ▲ Only applications that use stateful services must pay the overhead, in time and in code, of dealing with the status monitor.
- ▲ The implementation of stateful network applications is eased, since the status monitor shields application developers from the complexity of the network.

8

Remote Services

❑ Introduction

This chapter describes user programs that enable you to perform operations on remote hosts by using the TCP/IP networking software, which is part of the System V Release 4.0. A remote command is a command which runs on a machine other than the one you are using. Remote commands allow you to access machines of different architectures even if they are not running the same operating system. TCP/IP must be running for any of the commands described in this chapter to work.

The following topics are covered:

- ▲ Copying files from one machine to another with the `rcp` command.
- ▲ Executing commands on a machine other than the one you are currently logged in to, using the `rsh` command.
- ▲ Logging in to another UNIX system machine with the `rlogin` command.
- ▲ Logging in to another machine that does not run the UNIX operating system with the `telnet` command.

- ▲ Transferring files between different machines interactively using the `ftp` command and noninteractively using the `tftp` command.
- ▲ Logging in to remote machines by means of the `rlogin` command.
- ▲ Logging in to a machine running another operating system by means of the `telnet` command.
- ▲ Obtaining information about other users using the `finger` command.
- ▲ Determining if other machines are up and running using the `ping` command.

❑ Copying Files Between Machines

The `rcp` program copies files between your home machine and a remote machine. It has the form

`rcp` *source destination*

where

source	is the machine on which the file is located.
destination	is the machine to which the file is copied.

A detailed description of the arguments to `rcp` is provided in the sections that follow.

Copying Remote Files with **`rcp`**

To copy a file from a remote machine to your machine with `rcp`, use the following syntax:

`rcp` *machinename:file directory*

where

machinename	is the name of the machine from which to copy.
file	is the file to be copied.
directory	is the location on your system to which the copy is made.

For example, to copy the file `/home/dover/new.game` from the machine `pluto` to the directory `/home/baltimore/games` on the machine, `venus`, type

```
rcp pluto:/home/dover/new.game /home/baltimore/games
```

The standard UNIX shorthand for directory names applies when using `rcp`: for example, `$HOME` for your home directory when using the Bourne shell, a period (`.`) for the current directory, and two successive periods (`..`) for the parent of the current directory.

When copying a remote file, you can choose to rename that file on your home machine. To do so, specify the desired destination *filename* at the end of the destination directory on the home machine. For example, to copy the file `new.game` from machine `pluto` to your home directory and rename it `my.game`, type

```
rcp pluto:/home/dover/new.game $HOME/my.game
```

Copying Files to a Remote Machine with **rcp**

To copy a file from your machine to a remote machine using `rcp`, reverse the order of the arguments that from shown in the preceding section, as follows:

`rcp` *file machinename:directory*

where

file	is the file on your machine to be copied.
machinename	is name of the machine to which to copy.
directory	is the location to which the copy is made.

For example, to copy the file `/home/albany/old.game` from your home machine to the directory `/home/atlanta/stuff` on the machine `pluto`, type

```
rcp /home/albany/old.game pluto:/home/salem/stuff
```

To give the file a new name on the remote machine, specify a destination file name at the end of the destination directory on that machine. For example, typing

```
rcp /home/albany/old.game pluto:/home/salem/stuff/game
```

copies the file `old.game` from `/home/albany` directory to the file named `game` in the directory `/home/salem/stuff` on the machine `pluto`.

Copying Directories with `rcp`

To copy a directory and its contents from another machine to your machine, use `rcp` with the `-r` option. Otherwise the command works as it does for copying files if you replace the file names with the appropriate directory names.

The syntax for this command is

`rcp -r` *machinename*`:`*directory local_directory*

where

machinename	is the name of the remote machine.
directory	is the directory on the remote machine that you want to copy.
local_directory	is the directory on your machine to which the copy is made.

◆ ***Note*** Copying directories with `rcp` does not preserve ownership settings nor does it necessarily preserve permissions.

To copy a directory and its contents from your machine to another machine, the syntax is

`rcp -r` *local_directory machinename* **:** *directory*

where

local_directory	is the directory on your machine to be copied.
machinename	is the name of the remote machine
directory	is the location on the other machine to which the copy is made.

Error Messages

When attempting a remote copy, you may not have the proper permissions necessary to perform the operation. In such cases, you will get the error message `....Permission denied`, indicating that one of the following holds:

- ▲ You do not have read permission on the file you want to copy.
- ▲ You do not have write permission on the directory to which you want to copy.
- ▲ You do not have permission to access files in the remote machine because your machine's name is not in the remote machine's list of trusted hosts.

The message `Login incorrect` indicates you do not have permission to access files in the remote machine because your name is not in that machine's password database.

If you receive an error message, consult your system administrator.

❑ Executing Commands Remotely

The `rsh` (remote shell) command allows you to execute a single command on another machine without having to log in formally. `rsh` is an interpreter capable of executing commands on another machine. Using `rsh` can save time when you want to do only one thing on the remote machine.

To execute a command on another machine, type `rsh` followed by the machine's name and the command name. For example, to see the contents of the directory `/home/fresno/crops` on the machine `fresno`, type

```
rsh fresno ls -C /home/fresno/crops
```

When you use `rsh` to execute a command on another machine, `rsh` does not log in. Rather it talks to a daemon that spawns a shell and executes the command on the other machine. The type of shell spawned depends on the configuration of your entry in the remote machine's password database. If the shell spawned is the Bourne shell, your `.profile` file on the remote machine is read. If the shell is the C shell, your `.cshrc` file is read, if present, and `rsh` will use any pertinent aliases defined on the remote machine when executing the command.

Like `rlogin` and `rcp`, `rsh` uses the remote machine's password database and the files `/etc/hosts.equiv` and `.rhosts` to determine whether you have unchallenged access privileges.

`rsh` *and the Expansion of Shell Metacharacters*

With `rcp`, any shell metacharacters that are not escaped or in quotes are expanded at the local level, not at the level of the remote machine.

This caveat applies also to the redirection characters, `>`, `<`, and `|`. For instance, if you enter on machine `oak` the command

```
rsh willow ls /etc > /tmp/list
```

the output of the `ls` command on machine `willow` is redirected to a file `/tmp/list` on machine `oak`; but if you enter the command

```
rsh willow ls /etc '>' /tmp/list
```

the output is redirected to a file `/tmp/list` on machine `willow`, because the redirection is no longer at the local level.

Calling **rsh** *with No Commands*

If you call `rsh` using the syntax

`rsh` *machinename*

that is, with no arguments after the name of the remote machine, `rsh` behaves exactly as if you had entered

`rlogin` *machinename*

and you will be logged in at the remote machine, assuming you have permission.

Calling **rsh** *by a Different Name*

The command `rsh` can be called under a different name by making a symbolic link between the file `/usr/bin/rsh` and a file called by the name of the remote host.

For example, to create a symbolic link between `rsh` and a remote host called `willow`, enter the command

```
ln -s /usr/bin/rsh /usr/hosts/willow
```

Now, assuming the directory `/usr/hosts` is in your search path, you can enter the command

```
willow
```

on your machine to log in to machine `willow`.

To obtain a listing of the directory `/etc` on machine `willow`, enter

```
willow ls /etc
```

This process can be repeated for all the machines you frequently access remotely. Making the symbolic links in the directory `/usr/hosts` is a convention. You can make them in any directory, as long as you have permission to create files in that directory and it is in your search path.

❑ Transferring Files Between Machines

Files can be transferred between machines interactively by means of the `ftp` program or noninteractively, with the need to connect to the remote machine, by means of the `tftp` program.

Using `ftp` *to Interactively Transfer Files*

The `ftp` program copies files to and from machines on a network. To use `ftp`, you need not be a user on the remote machine, nor does the remote machine need to be running the same operating system. This command is also useful when you want to transfer files with unknown filenames, as `ftp` allows you to list directory contents on remote machines.

When you start `ftp`, you begin an interactive session with the daemon on the remote machine. The daemon is the part of the `ftp` program on the remote machine. It handles all that needs to be done on that end. Once you are connected, the daemon reports that the connection is established and then asks you to log in. If you have an entry in the password database on the remote machine, you can press **Return** to give the default response, your own username. When you enter the correct password, you will then be given access to files on that machine. A sample of such a login is shown in Figure 8-1.

```
venus$ ftp avignon
Connected to avignon.
220 avignon FTP server ready.
Name (avignon:stein):
Return
331 Password required for stein.
Password: (Here you type your password.)
230 User stein logged in.
ftp>
```

Figure 8-1: Sample* `ftp` *Login

For security reasons, the password does not echo on the screen when entered.

If you want to transfer files to or from a machine on which you do not have an entry in the password database, you can do so if the remote machine is set up for "anonymous" `ftp`. To set up a machine to allow anonymous `ftp`, create a login for `ftp` in your `/etc/passwd` file. Then make sure you have the directories and files shown in Figure 8-1 on your system.

Figure 8-2: Setting Up a Machine to Allow Anonymous **ftp**

File or Directory	Permissions	Owner
/home/ftp	dr-x--x--x	ftp
/home/ftp/bin	d--x--x--x	root
/home/ftp/bin/ls	---x--x--x	root
/home/ftp/dev	d--x--x--x	root
/home/ftp/dev/tcp	crw-rw-rw-	root
/home/ftp/dev/zero	crw-rw-rw-	root
/home/ftp/etc	d--x--x--x	root
/home/ftp/etc/group	-r--r--r--	root
/home/ftp/etc/netconfig	-r--r--r--	root
/home/ftp/etc/passwd	-r--r--r--	root
/home/ftp/pub	drwxrwxrwx	ftp
/home/ftp/usr	d--x--x--x	root
/home/ftp/usr/lib	d--x--x--x	root
/home/ftp/usr/lib/libc.so.1	-r-xr-xr-x	root

The `passwd` file above should have only entries for the `ftp` user and, perhaps, `root`, thus hiding the names of real users from anyone using anonymous `ftp`. If a file is owned by a user not listed in the `passwd` file, `ls` will display the UID instead of the name. The `tcp` and `zero` device nodes should be made with the `mknod (1M)` command using the same values that are in `/dev/tcp` and `/dev/zero`.

An anonymous `ftp` session might look as shown in Figure 8-3.

```
venus$ ftp berg
Connected to berg.
220 berg FTP server ready.
Name (berg:stein): anonymous
331 Guest login ok, send ident as password.
Password: (Here you type some identification string.)
User anonymous logged in.
ftp>
```

Figure 8-3: Anonymous `ftp` *Session*

Notice the request, `send ident as password`. The request indicates that there is no specific password, but that you should send some sort of identification as a password (your name, for example). After connection has been established, you are given the `ftp` prompt, indicating that `ftp` is ready to accept transfer commands.

Obtaining a Listing of Files on the Remote Machine

Once you are connected to a remote `ftp` daemon, you can list the files on the remote machine with the command `ls`. All accessible files in that directory will be listed. It is possible to move from one directory to another on the remote machine by means of the `cd` command. Unless you have access to the listed files, however, you will not be able to transfer them.

Copying Files Using `get` and `put`

The two commands most commonly used with `ftp` are `get` and `put`. These commands get a copy of a file from a remote machine or put a copy onto a remote machine, respectively. To use either command, enter the command followed by *filename*, the name of the file to be copied. The `ftp` program reports when the transfer begins and when the transfer is complete, along with diagnostic data indicating how long the transfer took. Figure 8-1 illustrates a typical transfer session.

Figure 8-4: Transferring Files with **`ftp`**

```
ftp> get lab1.results
200 PORT command successful.
150 ASCII data connection for lab1.results
(129.144.60.88,1163).
226 ASCII Transfer complete.
local: lab1.results remote: lab1.results
1162 bytes received in 0.08 seconds (14 Kbytes/s)
ftp>
ftp> put lab5.data
200 PORT command successful.
150 ASCII data connection for lab5.data (129.144.60.88,1165).
226 Transfer complete.
local: lab5.data remote: lab5.data
1162 bytes sent in 0.04 seconds (28 Kbytes/s)
ftp>
```

Copying Multiple Files Using `mget` and `mput`

You can "get" and "put" more than one file at a time using the commands `mget` and `mput`, along with metacharacters that can be used to specify multiple file names. For example, the metacharacter `*` will match anything, while `?` will match any single character. As with `get` and `put`, `ftp` reports when a transfer begins. Before each file is transferred, you are asked to confirm the operation. A "y" answer and the file is transferred; an "n" answer and the file is skipped. After all matching files have been transferred, the `ftp` prompt reappears. Figure 8-1 shows a typical transfer session with `mget` and `mput`.

```
ftp> mput lab*
mput lab1.results? y
200 PORT command successful.
150 ASCII data connection for lab1.results
(129.144.60.88,1180).
226 Transfer complete.
local: lab1.results remote: lab1.results
31 bytes sent in 0.02 seconds (1.5 Kbytes/s)
mput lab2.data? n
mput lab3.results? y
200 PORT command successful.
150 ASCII data connection for lab3.results
(129.144.60.88,1181).
226 Transfer complete.
local: lab3.results remote: lab3.results
75 bytes sent in 1e-06 seconds (7.3e+04 Kbytes/s)
ftp>
ftp> mget report?.final
mget report1.final? y
200 PORT command successful.
150 ASCII data connection for report1.final
(129.144.60.88,1195).
226 ASCII Transfer complete.
local: report1.final remote: report1.final
2605 bytes received in .44 seconds (5.8 Kbytes/s)
mget report2.final? n
```

***Figure 8-5: Transferring a File with* `mget` *and* `mput`**

Quitting an `ftp` Session

To terminate an `ftp`, session, enter the `quit` command at the prompt. The connection to the remote daemon will be dropped, and you will be returned to your local shell.

Aborting `ftp` While Transferring a File

If you are transferring files to or from a remote machine and that machine goes down, you should abort the transfer. To abort `ftp` when transferring a file, press the interrupt key—usually BREAK. You will be notified that the transfer was aborted and then given an `ftp` prompt again.

What Happens If No Daemon Is Present?

If the `ftp` daemon dies for any reason or if the machine you are communicating with never started one in the first place, you can still use `ftp`, but the session will be noninteractive. When this situation arises, `ftp` behaves like `tftp`, described in the next section.

Transferring Files Noninteractively Using `tftp`

The `tftp` program is very much like `ftp`, except that it is not an interactive process. With `tftp` you need not connect to the remote machine.When you begin a `tftp` session, you issue commands that directly copy files to and from the remote machine, assuming that you have an entry in the password database on the remote machine. Since the connection is not maintained between file transfers, no directory information is available from the remote machine.

To use `tftp`, enter the command

```
tftp
```

The prompt `tftp>` signals that the program is running and awaiting commands.

Obtaining Files Using `get`

To copy a file from the remote machine with `tftp`, use the command `get`. The syntax is

`get` *machinename*:*file* *

where

machinename	is the machine from which you wish to get the files.
file	is the name of the file to get.

More than one file can be placed on the command line, with spaces separating the file names.

Copying Files Using `put`

To copy a file to a remote machine, use the command `put`. The syntax for `put` is

`put` *machinename*`:`*file* * `[` *remote_directory* `]`

where

machinename	is the machine to which to transfer the files.
file	is the file name or a space-separated list of file names to transfer.
remote_directory	is an optional argument showing the specific directory on the remote machine into which you wish the files are to be placed.

Quitting a tftp Session

To leave the `tftp` program, enter the command `quit` at the prompt.

❑ Logging In to Remote Machines

When logging in to a remote machine, a key distinction is made between UNIX and non-UNIX machines. To log in to a UNIX machine, use the `rlogin` command. In the case of a non-UNIX machine, use the `telnet` command.

Logging into Another UNIX Machine

The `rlogin` command allows you to log in to other UNIX machines on a network. The command has the form

```
rlogin machinename
```

where *machinename* is the name of the machine to log in to.

If your machine's name is in the remote machines `/etc/hosts.equiv` file or in the `.rhosts` file in your remote home directory, the other machines trust your machine name and will not require you to type your password. Otherwise, a password prompt appears. Type your password followed by **Return**. If you have an entry in the password database of the remote machine and you enter the correct password, you will be logged in to the other machine as if you were the local machine.

A sample `rlogin` session is shown in Figure 8-6 below. Here, `rlogin` is used to remotely log in to the machine `jupiter` from the machine `venus`. Once remotely logged in, a `pwd` command is executed. This remote session is then terminated with the `exit` command. The system responds with the `connection closed` message.

Figure 8-6: Sample* `rlogin` *Session

```
venus$ rlogin jupiter
Password (Type your password here)
Last login: Mon Oct 21 00:30:52 from venus
jupiter$ pwd
/home/medici
jupiter$ exit
Connection closed.
venus$
```

Who Can Log in Remotely?

A user without an entry in the password database of a given machine is automatically denied permission to log in to that machine. If the user is listed in the password database, he or she will be asked for a password. If the password given matches the one in the database, permission to log in will be granted.

If the machine is listed in `/etc/hosts.equiv` on the remote host or if the user has an `.rhosts` file located in his or her remote home directory with the machine name listed in it, the user can log in without first supplying a password.

If you cannot `log in` to a remote machine because the machine identifies your password as incorrect, contact your systems administrator.

Remote Log In to a Machine as Someone Else

From time to time you may want to log into a remote machine under a different user name than the one used on the local machine at which you are working. This might be the case, for example, when you are working on another user's machine (under that user's username) and you want to log in to your own machine as yourself. By using your own username, you gain full access to your files. The `-l` option to `rlogin` allows you to do this. To log in to a remote machine under your own user another user name type

`rlogin` *machinename* `-l` *username*

where

machinename	is the name of the machine you wish to log in to.
username	is the username you wish to work under.

If the `-l` option is not specified, it is assumed that you wish to use your local username.

Aborting a Remote Connection

Sometime it may not be possible to terminate an `rlogin` connection using `exit` or `logout`. In such cases, you can abort the connection. To abort an `rlogin` connection, type a tilde character followed by a period (`~.`) at the beginning of a line. The connection to the other machine aborts, and you find yourself back at your original machine.

If you log in to a series of machines, accessing each machine through another machine, and you use ~. to abort the connection to any of the machines in the series, you return to the machine from which you started. All of the intermediate connections are severed.

In Figure 8-7, an `rlogin` connection is made from the machine `venus` to the machine `pluto`. From `pluto` the same connection is made to the machine `saturn`. When the abort command is issued, the user is returned not to `pluto` but to the machine from which the series of connections originated, `venus`.

Figure 8-7: Aborting an `rlogin` *Connection*

```
venus$ rlogin pluto
Last login: Wed July 28 05:04:01 from venus
pluto% rlogin saturn
Last login: Mon Jan 5 02:00:02 from pluto
pluto% ~.
Closed connection.
venus$
```

To disconnect to an intermediate `rlogin`, use two tildes followed by a period (`~~.`), as shown in Figure 8-8 below.

```
venus$ rlogin pluto
pluto% rlogin saturn
saturn% ~~ (Sometimes ~~ will not echo.)
pluto$
```

Figure 8-8: Disconnecting an Intermediate **rlogin**

Suspending an rlogin Connection

If you are using a job control shell (`jsh` or `ksh`), you can suspend an `rlogin` connection and return to it later. To do so, type the tilde character (~) followed by **Ctrl-Z**. The `rlogin` connection becomes a stopped process, and you are returned to the machine from which you logged in. To reactivate the connection, type `fg` or `%` followed by the job number of the stopped process. The default job number for `%` is the job you most recently stopped or put in the background.

Figure 8-9 illustrates the suspension of a remote connection.

```
venus$ rlogin earth
Last login: Thu Nov 21 07:07:07 from venus
earth$ ~ (Sometimes ^Z does not echo on the screen.)

Stopped
venus$ pwd
/home/nyc
venus$ fg
rlogin earth (Type Return here to get the command prompt.)

earth$ logout
Connection closed.
venus%
```

Figure 8-9: Suspending a Remote Connection

As is the case with aborting `rlogin` with ~~, using two tildes and a **Ctrl-Z** suspend you to an intermediate `rlogin`. For example, if from `oak` you `rlogin` to `willow` and from there to `cypress`, entering ~. brings you back to `oak`, but entering ~~. brings you back to `willow`.

Logging into a Machine Running Another Operating System

As `rlogin` only allows you to log in from one UNIX machine to another, you must use `telnet` to log in to a machine running a different operating system.

The `telnet` command communicates with another host by means of the TELNET protocol. If `telnet` is invoked without arguments, it enters command mode, as indicated by its prompt `telnet>`. In this mode, `telnet` accepts any of the commands listed below.

Logging in with `telnet`

The `telnet` command has the form

`telnet [` *host* `[` *port* `] ]`

where

host	is the name of the machine to connect to.
port	is the port number to use.

If no port is specified, `telnet` will attempt to contact a TELNET server at the default port.

Imagine that you want to log in to machine tops20 running the TOPS20™ operating system. To do so, type telnet followed by the machine name. The telnet program notifies you of the connection with the other machine and then identifies your escape character. At this point, you can log in to the remote machine as you ordinarily would. Establishing such a remote connection is shown in Figure 8-10.

```
venus$ telnet tops20
venus$ telnet tops20
Trying...
Connected to tops20.
Escape character is '^]'.


Acme Corp., TOPS-20 Monitor 6.1 (6762)-4
@LOG SATURN
```

Figure 8-10: Establishing a Remote Connection with **`telnet`**

If you attempt to log in to a machine that is not part of your network, telnet displays a notification and the telnet> prompt. To exit, type quit or the abbreviation q.

Suspending a `telnet` Connection

If you are using a job control shell (jsh or ksh), you can suspend a telnet connection and return to that connection later. To do so, type the standard escape character (usually **Ctrl-]**), followed by a z at the telnet prompt. At this point, the telnet program becomes a background process. To reactivate the connection, type fg, or % followed by the job number of the background process. The default job number for % is the job you most recently put in the background.

Figure 8-11 illustrates the process of suspending a telnet connection.

Figure 8-11: Suspending a `telnet` *Connection*

```
venus$ telnet tops20
venus$ telnet tops20
Trying...
Connected to tops20.
Escape character is '^]'.


Acme Corp., TOPS-20 Monitor 6.1 (6762)-4
@LOG SATURN

...
@ (Type Ctrl-] to get the telnet> prompt)
telnet> z

Stopped
venus% fg
telnet tops20 (Type Return twice to get the command prompt of the remote system)

@
```

Aborting a `telnet` Connection

A `telnet` connection should be aborted only when you cannot terminate the connection by means of `exit` or `logout` at the end of a work session. To abort a `telnet` connection, use the `telnet` escape character (generally **Ctrl-]**, followed by `quit` at the `telnet>` prompt. At this point, the login connection to the other machine will abort and you will find yourself back at your original machine.

If you log into a series of machines, accessing each machine through another machine, and you abort the connection to any of the machines in the series, you will return to the machine where you originally started, as shown in Figure 8-12.

```
venus$ telnet tops20
venus$ telnet tops20
Trying...
Connected to tops20.
Escape character is '^]'.


Acme Corp., TOPS-20 Monitor 6.1 (6762)-4
@LOG SATURN


...
@  (Type Ctrl-] to get the telnet> prompt)
telnet> quit
venus$
```

Figure 8-12: Aborting a `telnet` *Connection*

❑ Obtaining Information

Displaying User Information with `finger`

The `finger` command displays information about a specified user, accepting either a real name or a username as an argument. `finger` gives no information about other machines.

`finger` tells you:

- ▲ The user's login name.
- ▲ The user's real name.
- ▲ The user's home directory and login shell.
- ▲ The last time the user logged in to the machine from which you are issuing the command.
- ▲ The last time the user received mail, and the last time the user read it.
- ▲ The name of the user's terminal(s), and how long it has been idle.

Figure 8-13 presents a slightly simplified example of two typical `finger` requests. The first asks for information about the username `moby`. The second asks about user `Nathan Detroit`. Your output may vary somewhat.

Figure 8-13: Example **`finger`** *Session*

```
venus$ finger moby@sea
[sea]
Login name: moby          In real life: Ishmael Wong
Directory: /home/shipwreck/moby        Shell: /usr/bin/sh
On since Nov 14 06:33:41 on console   4 days 14 hours Idle
Time
New mail received Wed Nov 18 20:34:02 1987;
 unread since Wed Nov 18 16:20:24 1987
venus$ finger Nathan Detroit
Login name: nat         In real life: Nathan Detroit
Directory: /home/nyc/nat          Shell: /usr/bin/sh
Last login Wed Oct 21 16:16 on ttyp0 from broadway
No unread mail
```

The `finger` command allows you to determine whether a user you are looking for is still active. In the first case, user Ishmael Wong is logged in but has been idle for more than 4 days. In contrast, Nathan Detroit is not logged in.

Determining If a Machine Is Alive on the Network by Using **`ping`**

From time to time you may find that a remote machine is not answering your requests. This can indicate network-wide problems or simply that the host is down or disconnected from the network. The `ping` command offers the simplest way to find out if a host on your network is down. Its basic syntax is:

`/usr/bin/ping` *host* `[` *time-out* `]`

where *host* is the name of the machine in question. The optional *time-out* argument indicates how long `ping` should persist in its attempt to reach the machine. The time is specified in seconds and is 20 seconds by default. The `ping (1)` manual page describes additional details.

If you type,

```
ping dylan
```

and you receive the message

```
dylan is alive
```

you know that `dylan` has responded to your `ping`. If, however, host `dylan` is down or disconnected from the network, you will receive the following message:

```
no answer from dylan
```

This response appears after the time-out interval has elapsed.

9

The NIS Service

❑ Introduction

NIS is a distributed name service designed to meet the administrative needs of large, diverse, and evolving computing communities. It is a mechanism for identifying and locating the objects and resources accessible to such a community. It provides a uniform, network-wide storage and retrieval method that is both protocol- and media-independent.

By running the NIS service, a system administrator can distribute administrative databases known as maps among a variety of machines and can update those databases from a centralized location in an automatic and reliable fashion. This ensures that all clients share the same databases in a consistent manner. Furthermore, use of the NIS `publickey` map makes it possible to run secure RPC and secure NFS across a network of machines.

This chapter explains how to administer the NIS distributed network lookup service. It describes:

- ▲ The NIS environment.
- ▲ Setting up the NIS service.
- ▲ Creating and updating NIS maps.

- Adding a NIS server.
- Handling NIS problems.
- Turning off the NIS service.

❑ The NIS Environment

The NIS service operates using information contained in NIS maps. Maps are non-ASCII files typically derived from ASCII files generally found in the `/etc` directory. Programs access NIS maps by their mapname. On a network running NIS, at least one NIS server per domain maintains a set of NIS maps for other hosts in the domain to query.

The Elements of the NIS Service

The NIS service is composed of maps, domains, daemons, and utilities as described in the sections that follow.

NIS Maps

NIS maps are one possible of implementation of System V Release 4.0 administrative databases. Another implementation is the ASCII files generally found in the `/etc` directory.

Information in NIS maps is organized in a format similar to System V Release 4.0 `dbm` files. The manual pages for `ypfiles(5)` and `dbm(3)` describe the `dbm` file format. Input to `makedbm` must be in the form of *key/value* pairs, where *key* is the first word of each line and *value* is whatever follows in that line. The pairs of keys and values are preserved in the NIS maps, so programs can use the keys to look up the values.

The input can be from a file or from standard input (as when modified through a script). See "Making the NIS Maps" on page 125.

After passing through `makedbm` the data is collected in non-ASCII form in two files, `mapname.dir` and `mapname.pag`, both found in the `/var/yp/`*domainname* directory.

System V Release 4.0 includes a default NIS map, `publickey.byname`, and a default makefile for that map.

The NIS Domain

A NIS domain is an arbitrary name that designates which machines use a common set of maps. Maps for each domain are located in a separate directory, `/var/yp/`*domainname*, on the NIS server. (See "NIS Servers" on page 117.) For example, the maps for machines that belong to the domain `accounting` will be located in the directory `/var/yp/accounting` on their corresponding NIS server.

No restrictions are placed on whether a machine can belong to a given domain. Assignment to a domain is made on a machine-by-machine basis by the system administrator logged in as superuser. It can be done in any of the following three ways:

- By modifying `/etc/rc2.d/s75ppc`.
- By modifying `/etc/master.d/kernel`.
- By entering the command `domainname` *name* where *name* is the name of the domain to which the machine will belong.

The NIS Daemons

The NIS daemons are as follows:

- `ypserv` is a daemon that runs on NIS servers with a complete set of maps. It looks up requested information. At least one `ypserv` daemon must be present on the network for NIS service to function.
- `ypbind` is the NIS binder daemon. It must be present on both clients and servers. It initiates binding by finding a `ypserv` process that serves maps within the domain of the requesting client. `ypserv` must run on each NIS server. `ypbind` must run on all servers and clients.
- `ypupdated` is the server process for changing map entries. It facilitates the updating of NIS information.

The NIS Utilities

The NIS utilities are as follows:

- `ypcat` displays the contents of a NIS map.
- `ypwhich` lists the name of a NIS server. It shows which NIS server a client currently is using for NIS services or, if invoked with the `-m` *mapname* option, which NIS server is the master for each of the maps.
- `ypmatch` finds a key in a map file.
- `ypinit` builds and installs a NIS database or initializes a client server.

  It automatically creates maps for a NIS server from files located in `/etc. ypinit`. It also constructs those initial maps that are not built from files in `/etc`, such as `ypservers`. Use `ypinit` to set up the master NIS server and the slave NIS servers for the first time, as well as to initialize all clients.
- `yppoll` gets the protocol version from server. It tells which version of a NIS map is running on a specified server. It also lists the master server for the map.
- `yppush` propagates data from a NIS master to a slave server. It copies a new version of a NIS map from the NIS master server to its slaves. It is run on the master NIS server.
- `ypset` sets binding to a particular server by telling a `ypbind` process to bind to a named NIS server. Use `ypset` with care.
- `ypxfr` transfers data from master to slave NIS server. It moves a NIS map from one server to another, using NIS itself as the transport medium. `ypxfr` can be run interactively, or periodically from a `crontab` file. It is also called by `ypserv` to initiate a transfer.
- `makedbm` creates a `dbm` file for a NIS map. It converts an input file into `dbm .dir` and `.pag` files— `dbm` files that NIS can use as maps. `makedbm -u` can be used to "disassemble" a map, allowing you to see the key/value pairs that comprise it.

The `make` utility is also useful when running the NIS service.

- `make` updates NIS maps by reading the makefile in `/var/yp`. You can use `make` to update all maps based on the files in `/etc` or to update individual maps. The manual page `ypmake(1M)` describes `make` functionality for NIS.

NIS Machine Types

There are three types of NIS machines: master servers, slave servers, and clients. Any machine can be a NIS client, but only machines with disks should be NIS servers, whether master or slave. Generally, servers are also clients.

NIS Servers

By definition, a NIS server is a machine with a disk that stores a set of NIS maps that it makes available to network hosts. The NIS server does not have to be the same machine as the file server, unless the file server is the only machine on the network with a disk.

As has been stated, NIS servers come in two varieties, master and slave. The machine designated as NIS master server contains the master set of maps that are updated as necessary. If there is only one NIS server on your network, designate it as the master server. Otherwise, designate the machine best able to propagate NIS updates with the least performance degradation.

You can designate additional NIS servers on your network as slave servers. A slave server has a complete copy of the master server's set of NIS maps. Whenever the master server's maps are updated, it propagates the updates among the slave servers. The existence of slave servers allows the system administrator to distribute evenly the load borne in answering NIS requests. Figure 9-1 shows the relationship between master, slaves, and clients.

Figure 9-1: The Relationship Between Master, Slave, and Client Servers

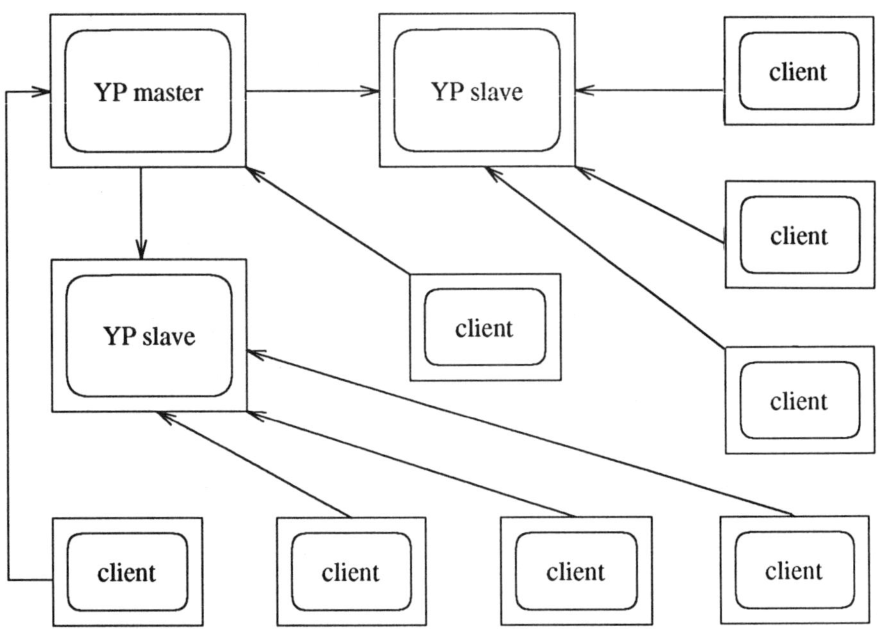

A server may be a master with respect to one map and a slave with respect to another. However, randomly assigning maps to NIS servers can cause a great deal of administrative confusion. It is best to designate a single server as the master for all the maps you create within a single domain. The examples in this chapter assume that one server is the master for all maps in the domain.

NIS Clients

NIS clients run processes that request data from maps on the servers. Clients do not care which server is the master in a given domain, since all NIS servers have the same information. The distinction between master and slave server only applies when making updates.

NIS Binding

NIS clients get information from the NIS server through the binding process. The following sequence of events take place during NIS binding:

1. A client process needing information that is normally provided by a NIS map asks `ypbind` for the name of a server.
2. `ypbind` gets a list of the servers for the domain from the file `/var/yp/binding/`*domainname*`/ypservers`. (See "Establishing the Domain" on page 120.)
3. `ypbind` initiates binding to the first server on the list. If that server does not respond, `ypbind` tries the next, and so on until it finds a server or exhausts the list.
4. `ypbind` informs the client process of the server name. The client then forwards its request directly to the server.
5. The `ypserv` daemon on the NIS server handles the request by consulting the appropriate map.
6. `ypserv` then sends the requested information back to the client.

The binding between a client and a server can change with the network's load as the service tries to compensate for current activity. That is, a client may get information from one server at one time and from another server at another time.

To find out which NIS server is currently providing service to a client, use the `ypwhich` command

```
$ ypwhich hostname
```

where *hostname* is the name of the client. If no *hostname* is mentioned, `ypwhich` defaults to the local host (the machine on which the command is entered).

❑ Setting Up the NIS Service

Setting up the NIS service requires the following steps:

1. Establishing the domain(s) for your machines.
2. Preparing the maps in ASCII form.
3. Running the ASCII files through `makedbm`.
4. Setting the master server.
5. Starting daemons in the master server.
6. Setting the slave server(s).
7. Starting daemons in the slave server(s).
8. Setup Up the NIS clients.

Each of these steps is described in the sections that follow.

Establishing the Domain

Before you configure machines as NIS servers or clients, you must prepare the NIS domain by:

- ▲ Giving it a name.

  A domain name can be up to 256 characters long. However, because your `/var/yp` directory may reside in an s5 file system and the domain name you select may be longer than the 14-character limit that s5 imposes on filenames, the program `ypinit` creates a shortened domain name and stores it in the `/var/yp/aliases` file. The name of the database directory `/var/yp/`*domainname* will correspond to the shortened alias for the domain name.

- ▲ Designating the machines that will serve or be served by the NIS domain.

  Once you have chosen a domain name, make a list of network hosts that will give or receive NIS service within that domain.

- ▲ Determining which machine should be master server.

  You can change this at a later date.

- ▲ Listing which hosts on the network, if any, are to be slave servers.
- ▲ Listing all the hosts that are to be NIS clients.

Although not strictly necessary, you will probably want all hosts in your network's administrative domain to receive NIS services. If this is the case, give the NIS domain the same name as the network administrative domain.

Log in as superuser on each server, whether master or slave(s), and all clients of the NIS domain. Enter the command

```
# domainname name
```

where *name* is the name of the domain.

The procedure described above is a temporary measure. Either edit the file in `/etc/rc2.d/s75rpc` that initiates the NIS service or edit the file `/etc/master.d/kernel`.

Preparing the Maps

System V Release 4.0 enables a site to use public key encryption as one of the methods for providing secure networking. If you are planning on running secure RPC or secure NFS, you can use the NIS service to administer the `/etc/publickey` file.

The `publickey` Map

Entries in the public key map file consists of three fields:

user name   *user public key* : *user secret key*

where

user name	may be the name of a user or of a machine.
user public key	is that key in hexadecimal notation.
user secret key	is that key also in hexadecimal notation.

The program newkey simplifies key generation. To use it, become superuser at the master server and type the following:

```
# newkey -u username
```

If superuser on a given host machine, type

```
# newkey -h hostname
```

At the prompt, enter the appropriate secure RPC or network password. The program will then create a new public/secret key pair in /etc/publickey, encrypted with the secure RPC or network password of the given user.

Users can later modify their own entries, or can even create them, by using the program chkey. The user types

```
$ chkey
```

and then responds to prompts from the command. A typical chkey session is shown in Figure 9-12.

Figure 9-2: **chkey** *Session*

```
willow$ chkey
Generating new key for username
Password: user enters password
Sending key change request to server...
Done.
willow$
```

For newkey and chkey to run properly, the daemon ypupdated must be running on the master server. If it is not running, enter the following:

```
# /usr/lib/netsvc/yp/ypupdated
```

You must also ensure that the appropriate file in /etc/rc?.d contains the lines

```
if [ -f /usr/lib/netsvc/yp/ypupdated -a -d \
     /var/yp/`domainname` ]
then
     /usr/lib/netsvc/yp/ypupdated
     (echo \c ' ypupdated') >/dev/console
fi
```

The ypupdated daemon consults the file /var/yp/updaters for information about which maps should be updated and how. In the case of the publickey map, changes to /etc/publickey affected through newkey or chkey are mediated by /usr/sbin/udpublickey.

Other Maps

Other maps do not need the assistance of special programs for their creation or modification. For instance, if you are planning to have distributed automounter files, write the automounter files as they would appear in a machine's /etc directory. For more information on the automounter, see the chapter "The Automounter" on page 39.

A typical auto.master file is shown in Figure 9-3.

```
#Mount-Point     Map                  Mount-options
/net             -hosts
/home            /etc/auto.home       -rw,intro,secure
/-               /etc/auto.direct     -ro,intr
```

Figure 9-3: **auto.master** *Map File*

A typical `auto.home` map might contain the entries shown in Figure 9-4.

Figure 9-4: **`auto.home`** *Map File*

```
#key        mount-options      location
willow                         willow:/home/willow
cypress                        cypress:/home/cypress
poplar                         poplar:/home/poplar
pine                           pine:/home/pine
apple                          apple:/home/apple
ivy                            ivy:/home/ivy
peach       -rw,nousid         peach:/home/peach
```

A typical `/etc/auto.direct` map is shown in Figure 9-5.

Figure 9-5: **`auto.direct`** *Map File*

```
/usr/local \
      /bin            -ro,soft     ivy:/export/local/sun4 \
      /share          -ro,soft     ivy:/export/local/share \
      /src            -ro,soft     ivy:/export/local/src
/usr/man              -ro,soft     rose:/usr/man \
                                   willow:/usr/map \
/usr/games            -ro,soft     peach:/usr/games
/usr/spool/news       -ro,soft     pine:/usr/spool/news
/usr/frame            -ro,soft     redwood:/usr/frame3.1 \
                                   balsa:/export/frame
```

A full description of automounter files can be found in Chapter 4, "The Automounter" on page 39.

These files are all found in the directory `/etc`. They are not the maps, but are the files used to create the maps.

The automounter recognizes the notation + at the beginning of a line as an indication to consult the corresponding NIS map. This notation is permissible in a client's file in the `/etc` directory.

Making the NIS Maps

Once created the ASCII map files must be converted into non-ASCII files in `dbm` format that the NIS service expects. The prescribed method is to use the `make(1)` program through a permanent makefile.

The Default Makefile

A makefile with the commands needed to transform `/etc/publickey` into the desired `dbm` format is provided in the directory `/var/yp`. That file is similar in format to the one shown in Figure 9-6.

Figure 9-6: Default Makefile

```
#ident"@(#)ypcmd:net_files/Makefile1.1"
#+++++++++++++++++++++++++++++++++++++++++++++++++++++++++++
#      PROPRIETARY NOTICE (Combined)
#
# This source code is unpublished proprietary information
# constituting, or derived under license from AT&T's UNIX(r)
System V.
# In addition, portions of such source code were derived from
Berkeley
# 4.3 BSD under license from the Regents of the University of
# California.
#
#      Copyright Notice
#
# Notice of copyright on this source code product does not
indicate
# publication.
#
#      (c) 1986,1987,1988.1989 Sun Microsystems, Inc
#      (c) 1983,1984,1985,1986,1987,1988,1989 AT&T.
#           All rights reserved.
#
# Set the following variable to "-b" to have yp servers use
the domain name
# resolver for hosts not in the current domain.
#B=-b
```

```
B=
DIR =/etc
DOM = `domainname`
NOPUSH = ""
YPDIR=/usr/sbin
YPDBDIR=/var/yp
YPPUSH=$(YPDIR)/yppush
MAKEDBM=$(YPDIR)/makedbm
MKNETID=$(YPDIR)/mknetid

all:      $(YPDBDIR)/$(DOM)/publickey.byname;

$(YPDBDIR)/$(DOM)/publickey.byname: $(DIR)/publickey
        sed "/^#/d" < $(DIR)/publickey | \
                $(MAKEDBM) - $(YPDBDIR)/$(DOM)/publickey.-
byname;
        echo "updated publickey";
        if [ ! $(NOPUSH) ]; then \
                $(YPPUSH) publickey.byname; \
                echo "pushed publickey"; \
      else \
      : ; \
      fi
```

Figure 9-6 Continued

This makefile first creates an entry in `/var/yp/aliases`. That entry translates the mapname into a shorter name to be used for the `dbm` file name. This is done to accommodate the 14-character limitation that s5 file systems impose on file names. Next, the makefile eliminates all lines in `/etc/publickey` that start with a **#**. That is, comment lines are eliminated. The rest is passed to `makedbm`.

`makedbm` creates the files `publickey.pag` and `publickey.dir`. Both of these files are in the directory `/var/yp/`*domain.name*. The makefile then touches a file called `publickey.time` to keep track of updates. The `yppush` program is called, if applicable, to propagate the changes to all slave servers.

It is inappropriate to call `make` until you have set the slave servers.

Modifying the Makefile

For the makefile to work on automounter files, or any other files that you wish to propagate through NIS, the following modifications must be made:

1. Modify the line

   ```
   all: publickey
   ```

   to read as follows:

   ```
   all: publickey auto.direct auto.home auto.master
   ```

   The order of the file names is not significant.

2. Add the following lines at the end of the makefile:

   ```
   auto.direct: auto.direct.time
   auto.home: auto.home.time
   auto.master: auto.master.time
   ```

3. Add the entry shown in Figure 9-7 for the `auto.direct` map in the middle of the file, after the entry for `publickey.time` and before the line that reads `publickey: publickey.time`.

```
auto.direct.time: $(DIR)/publickey
   -if [ -f $(DIR)/auto.direct ]; then \
      echo auto.direct.byname `$(ALIAS) publickey.byname` >>
$(ALIASFILE); \
      sort $(ALIASFILE) | uniq > .ypaliases; mv .ypaliases
$(ALIASFILE); \
      for i in $(DOM); do \
         sed -e "/^#/d" \
           -e s/#.*$$// \
           -e "/^ *$$/d" \
           -e "/^+/d" $(DIR)/auto.direct | \
         $(MAKEDBM) - $(YPDBDIR)/`$(ALIAS) \
           -d $$i`/`$(ALIAS) auto.direct.byname`; \
      done; \
      touch auto.direct.time; \
      echo "updated auto.direct"; \
      if [ ! $(NOPUSH) ]; then \
         $(YPPUSH) auto.direct.byname; \
         echo "pushed auto.direct"; \
      else \
         : ; \
      fi \
   else \
      echo "couldn't find $(DIR)/auto.direct"; \
   fi
```

Figure 9-7: Automounter Makefile

Create similar entries for `auto.home` and `auto.master`.

Setting the Master Server

The program `ypinit` helps to establish the master and slave servers and permits the initial mapping of ASCII files and their propagation. It is found in `/usr/sbin/ypinit`.

You use the shell script `ypinit` to build a fresh set of NIS maps on the master server in the following way:

1. Bring the machine that is going to be your master server to single-user mode or to a mode that is not defined as running the NIS service. Then log in as superuser.

2. Type

```
# cd /var/yp
# /usr/sbin/ypinit -m
```

3. `ypinit` prompts for a list of other hosts that are to become NIS servers. Enter the name of the server you are working on and the names of all other NIS servers.

4. `ypinit` asks whether you want the procedure to exit at the first non-fatal error or to continue despite non-fatal errors.

   If you choose the first option, `ypinit` will exit at the first problem. You can then fix the problem and restart `ypinit`. This option is recommended if you are running `ypinit` for the first time. If you prefer to continue, you can try to fix by hand all problems that occur, then restart `ypinit`.

   Once `ypinit` has constructed the list of servers, it calls `make(1)`. This program uses the instructions contained in the makefile (either the default one or the one you modified) located in `/var/yp`. It cleans all comment lines from the files you designated and runs `makedbm` on them, creating the appropriate pairs of maps and establishing the name of the master server for each map.

◆ ***Note*** For security reasons, you may wish to restrict access to the master NIS server.

Starting Daemons in the Master Server

The success of the remaining procedures depends on the presence of the `ypserv` daemon on the master server.

If your master server is still in single-user mode or at an inappropriate run level, bring it to the runlevel that will allow NIS services to run. Doing so entails ensuring that the lines shown in Figure 9-12, or similar lines, in the appropriate file in the `/etc/rc?.d` directory.

```
if [ -f /usr/lib/netsvc/yp/ypserv -a -d /var/yp/`domainname` ]
then
      /usr/lib/netsvc/yp/ypserv
      (echo \c ' ypserv') >/dev/console
fi
if [ -d /var/yp ]; then
      /usr/lib/netsvc/yp/ypbind
      (echo \c ' ypbind') >/dev/console
fi
```

Figure 9-8: Bringing Master Server to Run Level Allowing NIS Services to Run

Once you have ensured that these lines are in the file, that there is an executable file called `/usr/lib/netsvc/yp/ypserv` and a directory under `/var/yp` named after the domain name, log in as root and enter the command

```
# init #
```

where # is at least run level 2.

Setting Slave Servers

A network can have one or more NIS slave servers. Before actually running `ypinit` to create the slave servers, you should take several precautions.

- ▲ The domain name for each NIS slave must be the same as the domain name of the NIS master server.

  Use the `domainname` command on each NIS slave to make sure it is consistent with the master server. Make any necessary changes to the domain name, as described in the previous section, "Establishing the Domain" on page 120. Do not forget to set each slave server's host name.
- ▲ Make sure that the network is working properly before you set up a slave NIS server.

In particular, check that you can use `rcp` to send files from the master NIS server to NIS slaves. If you cannot, follow the procedures outlined in the "Copying Remote Files with rcp" on page 84 to permit the use of `rcp`.

Now you are ready to create a new slave server. To ensure that processes on the slave server actually use the NIS services, rather than files in the local `/etc` take the steps outlined below. In this way, you ensure that the NIS slave server is also a NIS client.

1. Log in to each slave server as superuser and bring the slave server to a run level, preferably single-user, that does not imply running the NIS service. `ypserv` must not be running.
2. Change directory to `/var/yp`.
3. Type

   ```
   # /usr/sbin/ypinit -c
   ```

   Enter the names of the NIS servers in order of preference; that is, enter first the names of the servers that are physically closest to the machine in the network. If the client is also a server, enter its name first. This step initializes the client and establishes its servers for binding.
4. Type

   ```
   # /usr/lib/netsvc/yp/ypbind
   ```

5. Type

   `# /usr/sbin/ypinit -s` *master*

   where *master* is the host name of the existing NIS master server. Ideally, the named host is the master server, but it can be any host with a stable set of NIS maps, such as another slave server.
6. `ypinit` will not prompt you for a list of other servers, as it does when you create the master server, nor will it run `make` again. However, it will stop executing if you have not used `ypinit -c` to initialize the list of servers, and it lets you choose whether or not to halt at the first non-fatal error. `ypinit` then calls the program `ypxfr`, which transfers a copy of the master's NIS map set to the slave server's `/var/yp/`*domainname* directory.
7. When `ypinit` terminates in each slave, make sure that the ASCII files in the `/etc` directory direct whichever program reads them to the NIS maps, thus ensuring homogeneity across the network. For

instance, if you have added the maps `auto.master`, `auto.home`, and `auto.direct` to the NIS maps, make a copy of each of these files in each slave by typing

```
# cp /etc/auto.home /etc/auto.home-
```

or

```
# cp /etc/auto.home /etc/auto.home.old
```

If the invocation does not contain the `-m` option, then the automounter will look for a NIS `auto.master` map. You can therefore move the `auto.master` file into another file:

```
# mv /etc/auto.master /etc/auto.master.orig
```

8. Edit the original files (not those with the `-` or `.old` extension) and make them refer to the NIS maps. For instance, the file `/etc/auto.direct` should contain, as its last line, something similar to the following:

   ```
   +auto.direct
   ```

   Whenever the automounter reads this file, it will consult the NIS `auto.direct` map upon reaching this line.

9. Back up copies of the edited files. To do so, you might type the following:

   ```
   # cp /etc/auto.direct /etc/auto.direct+
   ```

Repeat the procedures just described for each machine you want configured as a NIS slave server.

Starting Slave Server Daemons

The procedure for starting the NIS daemons in a slave server is exactly the same as that used for starting the NIS daemons in the master server, as explained in "Starting Daemons in the Master Server" on page 130.

Setting Up a NIS Client

To establish a machine as a NIS client, take the following steps:

1. Edit the client's local files, as you did for the local files in the slave servers, so that processes consulting those files are sent to the NIS maps.
2. Run

   ```
   # /usr/sbin/ypinit -c
   ```

   to initialize the client.
3. Bring the client to the run level defined as permitting the running of NIS services, after making sure that the appropriate file in the `/etc/rc2.d/s75rpc` directory contains lines similar to the following:

   ```
   if [ -d /var/yp ]; then
         /usr/lib/netsvc/yp/ypbind
         (echo \c ' ypbind')     >/dev/console
   fi
   ```
4. Type

   ```
   # ps -ef | grep ypbind
   ```

   to confirm that `/usr/lib/netsvc/yp/ypbind` is running.

With the relevant files in `/etc` abbreviated and `ypbind` running, the processes on the machine will be clients of the NIS servers.

At this point, you must have configured a NIS server on the network and have given that server's name to `ypinit`. Otherwise, processes on the client will hang if no NIS server is available while `ypbind` is running.

❑ Administering NIS Maps

This section describes how to maintain the maps in an existing NIS domain. Subjects discussed include:

- ▲ Updating NIS maps.
- ▲ Propagating a NIS map.
- ▲ Adding new NIS maps to the makefile.

Updating Existing Maps

Some NIS maps require frequent updating while others never need to change. For example, the `publickey` map may change frequently on a large company's network. On the other hand, the `auto.master` map probably will change little, if at all.

When you need to update a map, you can use one of two update procedures, depending on whether the map is standard or nonstandard. A standard map is a map in the default set created by `ypinit` from the network databases. Nonstandard maps may be any of the following:

- ▲ A map included with an application purchased from a vendor.
- ▲ A map created specifically for your site.
- ▲ A map existing in a form other than ASCII.

The following text explains how to use various updating tools. In practice, you will use them only if you add nonstandard maps or change the set of NIS servers after the system is up and running.

Modifying Standard Maps

Always modify NIS maps on the master server. Use the following procedure to update all standard maps:

1. Become superuser on the master server.
2. Edit the file in `/etc` with the same name as the map you want to change.
3. Type the following:

```
# cd /var/yp
# make mapname
```

   The `make` command will then update the map according to the changes made in its corresponding file. It will also propagate the updated map among the servers. See the section "Propagating an NIS Map" on page 139 for more information.

◆ ***Note*** Do not use this procedure with the `publickey` map. Instead, use the `newkey` and `chkey` commands, as described in "Preparing the Maps" on page 121.

Creating and Modifying Nonstandard Maps

To update a nonstandard map, you edit its corresponding ASCII file. The updated map is then rebuilt using the `/usr/sbin/makedbm` command. (The `makedbm(1M)` manual page fully describes this command.) If the map to be rebuilt has an entry in the `/var/yp/Makefile,` simply run `make.` If the map does not have an entry, try to create one by following the instructions in "Making the NIS Maps" on page 125. Using `make` is the preferred method. Otherwise, you will have to use `makedbm` step-by-step.

There are two different methods for using `makedbm:`

▲ Redirect the command's output to a temporary file, modify that file, then use the modified file as input to `makedbm`.

▲ Direct the output of `makedbm` to be operated on within a pipeline that feeds back into `makedbm`. This method is appropriate if you can update the disassembled map with either `awk,` `sed,` or a `cat` append.

There are two possible procedures for creating new maps. The first uses an existing ASCII file as input; the second uses standard input.

If `/var/yp` resides in an s5 file system, you must create an alias for the map because of the 14-character limitation for file names. In the case of map names, this is actually an 8-character limitation because of the suffixes that `makedbm` creates. To create the alias, change the directory to `/var/yp` and enter the command:

```
echo mapname `/usr/lib/netsvc/yp/ypalias mapname` >> aliases
```

Updating Maps Built from Existing ASCII Files

Assume that an ASCII file `/var/yp/mymap.asc` was created with an editor or a shell script on the NIS master. You want to create a NIS map from this file and locate it in the `home_domain` subdirectory. To do so, type the following on the master server:

```
#   cd /var/yp
#   /usr/sbin/makedbm mymap.asc home_domain/mymap
```

The `mymap` map now exists in the directory `home_domain`.

Adding entries to `mymap` is simple. First, you must modify the ASCII file `mymap.asc`. If you modify the actual `dbm` files without modifying the corresponding ASCII file, the modifications are lost. Type the following:

```
#   cd /var/yp
#   <edit mymap.asc>
#   /usr/sbin/makedbm mymap.asc home_domain/mymap
```

When you finish updating the map, you must propagate it to the slave servers, as described in the section "Propagating an NIS Map" on page 139.

Updating Maps Built from Standard Input

When no original ASCII file exists, create the NIS map from the keyboard by typing input to `makedbm`, as shown in Figure 9-9.

Figure 9-9: Building a NIS Map from Standard Input

```
ypmaster# cd /var/yp
ypmaster# /usr/sbin/makedbm - home_domain/mymap
key1 value1
key2 value2
key3 value3
<ctl D>
ypmaster#
```

If later you need to modify a map that is not based on an existing file, you can use `makedbm -u` to disassemble the map and create a temporary ASCII intermediate file. To do so, type the following:

```
$  cd /var/yp
$  /usr/sbin/makedbm -u home_domain/mymap > mymap.temp
```

The resulting temporary file `mymap.temp` has one entry per line. You can edit it as needed.

To update the map, give the name of the modified temporary file to `makedbm` as follows:

```
$  /usr/sbin/makedbm mymap.temp home_domain/mymap
$  rm mymap.temp
```

When `makedbm` finishes, propagate the map to the slave servers, as described in the section "Propagating an NIS Map" on page 139.

The preceding paragraphs explained how to use some tools. In reality, unless you add nonstandard maps to the database or change the set of NIS servers after the system is already up and running, almost everything you have to do can be done by `ypinit` and `/var/yp/Makefile`.

Whether you use the makefile in `/var/yp` or some other procedure, a new pair of well-formed `dbm` files must end up in the domain directory on the master NIS server.

Propagating an NIS Map

When you propagate an NIS map, you move it from place to place—most often from the master to all NIS slave servers. Initially `ypinit` propagates the maps from master to slaves, as described previously. From then on, you must transfer updated maps from master to slaves by running the `ypxfr` command. You can run `ypxfr` in any of three different ways:

- Periodically through the root `crontab` file.
- By the `ypserv` daemon.
- Interactively on the command line.

`ypxfr` handles map transference in tandem with the `yppush` program. `yppush` should always be run from the master server. The makefile in the `/var/yp` directory automatically runs `yppush` after the master set of maps is changed.

`yppush` copies or "pushes," a new version of a NIS map from the NIS master to the slave servers. After making a list of NIS servers from the `ypservers` map built by `ypinit`, `yppush` contacts each slave server in the list and sends it a "transfer map" request. When the request is acknowledged by the slave, the `ypxfr` program transfers the new map to the slave.

Using `crontab` with `ypxfr`

Maps differ in how frequently they change. For instance, `auto.master` may not change for months at a time, but `publickey` may change several times a day in a large organization. When you schedule map transference through the `crontab` command, you can designate the intervals at which individual maps are to be propagated.

To run `ypxfr` periodically at a rate appropriate for your map set, edit root's `crontab` file on each slave server and put the appropriate `ypxfr` entries in it. See the manual page for `crontab(1)` for additional information. `ypxfr` contacts the master server and transfers the map only if the master's copy is more recent than the local copy.

Using Shell Scripts with `ypxfr`

As an alternative to creating separate `crontab` entries for each map, you can have root's `crontab` periodically run shell scripts that update the maps. These shell scripts can be easily modified to fit your site requirements or to replace them. A sample shell script is shown in Figure 9-10.

Figure 9-10: Updating NIS Maps with Shell Scripts

```
#! /bin/sh
#
# ypxfr_1perday.sh - Do daily yp map check/updates
#

# set -xv
ypxfr publickey.byname
ypxfr auto.direct
ypxfr ypservers
```

This shell script updates the mentioned maps once per day, so long as root's `crontab` executes it once a day (preferably at times of low network load). You can choose to have scripts update maps once a week, once a month, once every hour, and so on. If you do, be aware of the performance degradation implied in propagating the maps.

Run the same shell scripts through root's `crontab` on each slave server configured for the NIS domain. Alter the exact time of execution from one server to another to avoid overloading the master server.

To transfer the map from a particular slave server, use the `-h` *host* option of `ypxfr` within the shell script. The syntax of the commands you put in the script is

`/usr/lib/netsvc/yp/ypxfr -h` *host mapname*

where

host	is the name of the server with the maps you want to transfer.
mapname	is the name of the requested map.

If you use the `-h` option without specifying *host*, `ypxfr` will attempt to get the map from the master server.

Use the `-s` *domain* option to transfer maps from another domain to your local domain. These maps should be essentially be the same across domains.

Directly Invoking ypxfr

The third method of invoking `ypxfr` is to run it as a command. Typically, this is done only in exceptional situations—for example, when setting up a temporary NIS server to create a test environment or when trying to make a NIS server that has been out of service consistent with the other servers.

Logging ypxfr's Activities

`ypxfr`'s transfer attempts and the results can be captured in a log file. If a file called `/var/yp/ypxfr.log` exists, results are appended to it. No attempt is made to limit the size of the log file. Empty it from time to time by entering

```
# cp /var/yp/ypxfr.log /var/yp/ypxfr.log.old
# cat /dev/null > /var/yp/ypxfr.log
```

`crontab` can be used to execute these commands once a week. To turn off logging, remove the log file.

Adding New NIS Maps to the Makefile

Adding a new NIS map entails putting copies of the map's `dbm` files into the `/var/yp/`*domain_name* directory on each of the NIS servers in the domain. The actual mechanism is described in "Propagating an NIS Map" on page 139. This section only describes how to update the makefile so that propagation works correctly.

After deciding which NIS server is the master of the map, modify `/var/yp/Makefile` on the master server so that you can conveniently rebuild the map. As indicated previously, different servers can be masters of different maps. This can, however, lead to administrative confusion, and it is strongly recommended that you set only one server as the master of all maps. Case-by-case modification is too varied to describe here, but typically a human-readable ASCII file is filtered through `awk`, `sed`, and/or `grep` to make it suitable for input to `makedbm`. Refer to the existing `/var/yp/Makefile` for examples. See also, "Modifying the Makefile" on page 128.

Use the mechanisms already in place in `/var/yp/Makefile` when deciding how to create dependencies that `make` will recognize; specifically, the use of `.time` files allows you to see when the makefile was last run for the map.

To obtain an initial copy of the map, you can have `make` run `yppush` on the NIS master server. The map must be available globally before clients begin to access it.

◆ ***Note*** If the map is available from some, but not all, NIS servers you will encounter unpredictable behavior from client programs.

❑ Adding a New NIS Server

This section describes the procedures for adding a new NIS server. In particular, it describes the process of moving the master map set to a new server.

After NIS is running, you may need to create a NIS slave server that you did not include in the initial set given to `ypinit`. The following procedure explains how to do so:

1. Log in to the master server as superuser.
2. Go to the NIS domain directory by typing

```
# cd /var/yp/domain_name
```

3. Disassemble `ypservers`, as follows:

```
# /usr/sbin/makedbm -u ypservers > /tmp/temp_file
```

   `makedbm` converts `ypservers` from `dbm` format to the temporary ASCII file `/tmp/`*temp_file*.

4. Edit `/tmp/`*temp_file* using your preferred text editor. Add the new slave server's name to the list of servers. Then save and close the file.
5. Run the `makedbm` command with `temp_file` as the input file and `ypservers` as the output file.

```
# /usr/sbin/makedbm /tmp/temp_file ypservers
```

   Here `makedbm` converts `ypservers` back into `dbm` format.

6. Verify that the `ypservers` map is correct (since there is no ASCII file for `ypservers`) by typing the following:

```
ypslave# /usr/sbin/makedbm -u ypservers
```

◆ ***Note*** If a host name is not in **`ypservers`**, that host will not be warned of updates to the NIS map files.

   Here `makedbm` will display each entry in `ypservers` on your screen.

7. Set up the new slave server's NIS domain directory by copying the NIS map set from the master server. To do this, log in to the new NIS slave as superuser and run the `ypinit` command:

```
ypslave# cd /var/yp
ypslave# ypinit -c
< enter the list of servers >
ypslave# /usr/lib/netsvc/yp/ypbind
ypslave# /usr/sbin/ypinit -s ypmaster
```

   When you are finished, complete Steps 5 and 6 in "Setting Slave Servers" on page 131.

Changing a Map's Master Server

To change a map's master, you first have to build it on the new NIS master. The old master's name occurs as a key/value pair in the existing map (this pair is inserted automatically by makedbm). Therefore, using the existing copy as the new master or transferring a copy to the new master with ypxfr is insufficient. You have to reassociate the key with the new master's name. If the map has an ASCII source file, you should copy it in its current version to the new master.

For example, the instructions for remaking a sample NIS map jokes.bypunchline, are as follows:

1. Log in to the new master as superuser and type the following:

   ```
   newmaster# cd /var/yp
   ```

2. /var/yp/Makefile must have an entry for the new map before you specify the map to make. If this is not the case, edit the makefile to create the needed entry (see "Making the NIS Maps" on page 125).

3. Type the following:

   ```
   newmaster# make jokes.bypunchline
   ```

4. If the old master will remain a NIS server, use rlogin to connect to that server and edit /var/yp/Makefile. Comment out the section of /var/yp/Makefile that made jokes.bypunchline.

5. If jokes.bypunchline exists only as a dbm file, remake it on the new master by disassembling a copy from any NIS server, then running the disassembled version through makedbm:

   ```
   newmaster# cd /var/yp
   newmaster# ypcat -k jokes.bypunchline |\
   /usr/sbin/makedbm - domain/jokes.bypunchline
   ```

   jokes.bypunchline must also be in the alias file.

After making the map on the new master, you must send a copy of it to the other slave servers. However, do not use yppush, as the other slaves will try to get new copies from the old master, rather than from the new one. To circumvent this, transfer a copy of the map from the new master back to the old master. Become superuser on the old master server and type

```
oldmaster# /usr/lib/netsvc/yp/ypxfr -h newmaster
jokes.bypunchline
```

Now it is safe to run `yppush`. The remaining slave servers still believe that the old master is the current master. They will attempt to get the current version of the map from the old master. When they do so, they will get the new map, which names the new master as the current master.

If this method fails, you can try this cumbersome but sure-fire option: Log in as superuser on each NIS server and execute the `ypxfr` command shown above.

❑ Handling NIS Problems

This section explains how to clear problems encountered on networks running NIS. It has two parts:

- ▲ Debugging a NIS client.
- ▲ Debugging a NIS server.

Debugging a NIS Client

Before trying to debug a NIS client, review the first part of this chapter, which explains the NIS environment. Then look for the subheading in this section that best describes your problem. The subsections are as follows:

- ▲ Hanging commands on the client machine.
- ▲ NIS service is unavailable.
- ▲ `ypbind` crashes.
- ▲ `ypwhich` displays are inconsistent.

Hanging Commands on the Client

The most common problem of NIS clients occurs when a command hangs. Sometimes many commands begin to hang, even though the system as a whole seems normal and you can run new commands.You will see console messages such as

```
yp: server not responding for domain <domainname>.  Still trying
```

The message indicates that `ypbind` on the local machine is unable to communicate with `ypserv` in the domain *domainname.* This happens when a machine running `ypserv` has crashed or is down or otherwise unavailable. It may also occur if the network or NIS server is so overloaded that `ypserv` cannot get a response back to the client's `ypbind` within the time-out period.

Under these circumstances, every client on the network will experience the same or similar problems. The condition is temporary in most cases. The messages generally will stop when the NIS server reboots and restarts `ypserv` or when the load on the NIS server or network itself decreases.

However, hung commands may require direct action to clear. The following describes the causes of such problems and suggests solutions:

- The NIS client has not set, or has incorrectly set, the machine's domain name. Clients must use a domain name that the NIS servers know.

  On the client, type `domainname` to see which domain name is set. Compare that with the actual domain name in `/var/yp` on the NIS master server. If a machine's domain name is not the same as the server's, the machine's domain name entry in its installation scripts is incorrect. Log in as superuser, edit the client's installation scripts, and correct the `domainname` entry. This ensures the domain name is correct every time the machine boots. Then set `domainname` manually by typing the following:

  `# domainname` *good_domain_name*

- If commands still hang, make sure the server is up and running. Check other machines on your local network. If several clients also have problems, suspect a server problem. Try to find a client machine behaving normally. Type the `ypwhich` command on that client. If ypwhich does not respond, kill it and go to a terminal on the NIS server. Type the following:

```
ypserver# ps -ef | grep yp
```

Look for ypserv and ypbind processes. If a ypserv process is running, type

```
ypserver# ypwhich
```

on the NIS server. If ypwhich does not respond, ypserv has probably hung, and you should restart it. Type the following while logged in as superuser:

```
ypserver# kill -9 (ypserv's pid # from ps)
ypserver# /usr/lib/netsvc/yp/ypserv
```

If ps shows no ypserv process running, start one.

- ▲ If the server's ypbind daemon is not running, start it by typing the following:

  ```
  ypserver# /usr/lib/netsvc/yp/ypbind
  ```

  Notice that if you run ypbind and you type ypwhich immediately, ypwhich will always return the error message not found. Run ypwhich again; it should now return the name of a server.

- ▲ If commands still hang, try the following:

  1. Kill the existing ypbind:

     ```
     # ps -ef | grep ypbind
     ```

  2. Restart ypbind with the ypset option that permits root to change the server:

     ```
     # ypbind -ypsetme
     ```

  3. Reset the server to one you know is reliable:

     ```
     # ypset servername
     ```

NIS Service Is Unavailable

When most machines on the network appear to be behaving normally, but one client cannot receive NIS service, that client may experience many different symptoms. For example, some commands appear to operate correctly while others terminate with an error message about the unavailability of NIS.

Other commands execute slowly in a backup-strategy mode particular to the program involved. Still other commands or daemons crash with obscure messages or no message at all. Here are messages a client in this situation may receive:

```
$ ypcat myfile
ypcat: can't bind to NIS server for domain <domainname>.
        Reason: can't communicate with ypbind.
```

or

```
$ /usr/lib/netsvc/yp/yp/yppoll myfile
yppoll: Sorry, I can't communicate with ypbind.
I give up.
```

These symptoms usually indicate that the client's `ypbind` process is not running. Run `ps -ef` and check for `ypbind`. If it you do not find it, log in as superuser and type the following:

```
# /usr/lib/netsvc/yp/ypbind
```

NIS problems should disappear.

ypbind Crashes

If `ypbind` crashes almost immediately each time it is started, look for a problem in some other part of the system. Check for the presence of the `rpcbind` daemon by typing the following:

```
$  ps ax | grep rpcbind
```

If it is not running, reboot.

If `rpcbind` itself will not run or behaves strangely, look for more fundamental problems. Check the network software in the ways suggested in See Chapter 3, "Handling NFS Problems" on page 27..

You may be able to communicate with `rpcbind` on the problematic client from a machine operating normally. From the functioning machine, type

```
$ rpcinfo client | grep ypbind
```

If `rpcbind` on the problematic machine is running normally, `rpcinfo` should produce an output similar to that shown in Figure 9-11.

```
   100007   3     tcp  0.0.0.0.12.169  ypbind  superuser
   100007   3     udp  0.0.0.0.4.9  ypbind  superuser
   100007   3  ticlts  Q 00 00 00  ypbind  superuser
   100007   3  ticots   07 00 00 00  ypbind  superuser
   100007   3  ticotsord   07 00 00 00  ypbind  superuser
   100007   3  starlandg
00 15sfsc.30719?00 20I 00 00 00 00 00 00 00 10 \
      00j 10 32v\376 02  ypbind  superuser
   100007   3  starlan
00 15sfsc.;3719?00 20I 00 00 00 00 00 00 00 10 \
      00j 10 32v\376 01  ypbind  superuser
```

Figure 9-11: Output from **`rpcbind`**

There should be one entry per transport; in the preceding example, the entry for `udp` is missing. Because `ypbind` was not registered for it in this case, `ypbind` cannot run on `udp`. As long as there are other transports to run on, `ypbind` should run, but the omission may indicate some kind of a problem. Reboot the machine and run `rpcinfo` again. If the `ypbind` processes are present and change each time you restart `/usr/lib/netsvc/yp/ypbind`, reboot the system, even if the `rpcbind` daemon is running.

`ypwhich` Displays Are Inconsistent

When you use `ypwhich` several times on the same client, the resulting display may vary because the NIS server changes. The changed display is normal. The binding of NIS client to NIS server changes over time when the network or the NIS servers are busy. Whenever possible, the network stabilizes at a point where all clients get acceptable response time from the NIS servers. As long as your client machine gets NIS service, it does not matter where the service comes from. For example, one NIS server machine can get its own NIS services from another NIS server on the network.

Debugging a NIS Server

Before trying to debug your NIS server, read about the NIS environment at the beginning of this chapter. Then look in this subsection for the heading that most closely describes the server's problem. The problems described are as follows:

- Servers have different versions of a NIS map.
- `ypserv` crashes.

Servers Have Different Versions of a NIS Map

Because NIS propagates maps among servers, occasionally you find different versions of the same map at NIS servers on the network. This version discrepancy is normal if transient, but abnormal if it persists.

Most commonly, normal map propagation is prevented if it occurs when a NIS server or router between NIS servers is down. When all NIS servers and the routers between them are running, `ypxfr` should succeed.

If a particular slave server has problems updating maps, log in to that server and run `ypxfr` interactively. If `ypxfr` fails, it will tell you why it failed, and you can fix the problem. If `ypxfr` succeeds, but you suspect it has occasionally failed, create a log file to enable logging of messages. As superuser, type the following:

```
ypslave# cd /var/yp
ypslave# touch ypxfr.log
```

This procedure saves all output from `ypxfr`. The output resembles the output that `ypxfr` displays when run interactively, but each line in the log file is time-stamped. You may see unusual orderings in the timestamps. This is normal— the time-stamp tells you when `ypxfr` started to run. If copies of `ypxfr` ran simultaneously but their work took different amounts of time, they may actually write their summary status line to the log files in an order different from that in which they were invoked. Any pattern of intermittent failure shows up in the log. When you have fixed the problem, turn off logging by removing the log file. If you forget to remove it, it will grow without limit.

While still logged in to the problem NIS slave server, inspect the root's `crontab` file and the `ypxfr*` shell scripts it invokes. Typing errors in these files cause propagation problems, as do failures to refer to a shell script within `/var/spool/cron/crontabs/root` or failures to refer to a map within any shell script.

Also, make sure that the NIS slave server is in the map `ypservers` within the domain. If it is not, it still operates perfectly as a server, but `yppush` will not tell it when a new copy of a map exists.

If the NIS slave server's problem is not obvious, you can work around it while you debug it with `rcp` or `tftp` to copy a recent version of the inconsistent map from any healthy NIS server. You must not do this remote copy as root, but you can do it while logged in as `daemon`. For instance, you might transfer the map `busted` using the method shown in Figure 9-12.

```
ypslave# chmod go+w /var/yp/mydomain
ypslave# su daemon
$ rcp ypmaster:/var/yp/mydomain/busted.\* /var/yp/mydomain
$ exit
ypslave# chown root /var/yp/mydomain/busted.*
ypslave# chmod go-w /var/yp/mydomain
```

Figure 9-12: Transferring a NIS Map File

Here the `*` character has been escaped in the command line so that it will be expanded on `ypmaster`, instead of locally on `ypslave`. Notice that the map files should be owned by root, so you must change their ownership after the transfer.

ypserv Crashes

When the `ypserv` process crashes almost immediately and will not stay up even with repeated activations, the debug process is virtually identical to that previously described in "ypbind Crashes" on page 148. Check for the existence of the `rpcbind` daemon as follows:

```
ypserver$ ps -ef | grep rpcbind
```

If you do not find the daemon, reboot the server. If the daemon is present, type

```
$ rpcinfo yp_server | grep ypserv
```

and look for output similar to that shown in Figure 9-13.

Figure 9-13: Output from **rpcinfo**

```
   100004    2     tcp  0.0.0.0.12.168  ypserv  superuser
   100004    2     udp  0.0.0.0.4.8  ypserv  superuser
   100004    2  ticlts  B 00 00 00  ypserv  superuser
   100004    2  ticots   06 00 00 00  ypserv  superuser
   100004    2  ticotsord   06 00 00 00  ypserv  superuser
   100004    2  starlandg
00 15sfsc.2>219?00 20I 00 00 00 00 00 00 00 10 \
      00j 10 32v\376 02  ypserv  superuser
   100004    2  starlan
00 15sfsc.31319?00 20I 00 00 00 00 00 00 00 10 \
      00j 10 32v\376 01  ypserv  superuser
```

Your machine will have different port numbers. As in the case of ypbind, there should be one entry per transport. If a transport is missing, ypserv has been unable to register its services with it. Reboot the machine. If the ypserv processes are there and they change each time you attempt to restart /usr/lib/netsvc/yp/ypserv, reboot the machine.

❑ Turning Off NIS Services

If ypserv on the master is disabled, none of the NIS maps can be updated. On the other hand, if no ypserv daemon is running but ypbind is running on clients, machines may hang indefinitely until they find a ypserv daemon.

To turn off NIS services safely, make sure no client is running ypbind before turning off ypserv in the master and slave servers.

Glossary

abort To discontinue a process without waiting for the normal exit. Aborting is normally achieved by sending an interrupt signal to the program you are running.

binding The process by which a client locates the server that shares the information desired and then sets up communication with that server.

caller process A process that uses RPC to have another process execute a procedure call.

client A machine that mounts resources shared by a server.

credential Information used to prove that something is as it claims to be—for example, an identification badge. See also *verifier.*

daemon A program that runs autonomously, performing actions that facilitate more complex operations. Many remote commands get information from a remote machine by exchanging data with daemons running on the remote machine. The mail service is a daemon that processes mail automatically and routes it to the intended recipient.

Data Encryption Standard (DES) A standard cryptography algorithm used to ensure data security.

diskless client A machine that has no local disk and is, therefore, dependent upon the server for all its file storage. Diskless machines can act only as clients, never as servers.

domain An administrative entity, typically consisting of several machines, that joins a larger network.

file handle A key obtained by a client from a server to facilitate all further requests between that client and server.

group identification number (GID)
A number that refers to a specific group of users on a system. Each user can belong to one or more groups.

hierarchy All or part of a file structure including the directories and the files within the structure.

host An individual machine.

hang To stop abnormally without the capability of being restarted.

local machine The machine you are currently logged in to as opposed to a *remote* machine.

map A file containing a listing of mount points and their corresponding resources. The maps are used by the automounter program to locate where a file structure should be mounted when it is needed.

mount The action a client performs to access files in a server's shared directories. When a client mounts a resource, it does not copy that resource, but rather transparently accesses the resource as if it were local.

mount point The location within the directory tree through which a machine accesses a mounted resource. The mount point for a resource is usually an empty directory.

netname A string of printable characters created by concatenating the name of the operating system, a user ID, and a domain name. Netnames are used in DES authentication.

Network File System (NFS)
A service that enables machines to share file resources across a network.

NIS Distributed name service used to identify and locate objects and resources accessible to a computing community. It provides a uniform, network-wide storage and retrieval method that is both protocol- and media-independent.

NIS Server A machine with a disk that stores a set of NIS maps that it makes available to network hosts.

process identification number (PID)
A number that identifies a process to the operating system. Every process has a PID by which it is referenced.

public key cryptography
A cipher system that uses a published public key and an encoded secret key.

remote machine
The machine to which you are connected across the network.

Remote Procedure Call (RPC)
Procedures that provide the means by which one process (the *caller*) can have another process (the *server*) execute a procedure call as if the caller had done so itself locally.

resource A file system, a portion of a file system, a directory, or a single file shared by a server across a network.

run level A user mode, also called a *run state*.

server A machine that shares file systems or portions of file systems, allowing remote machines to mount those resources.

server process A process that receives directives from a *caller process* to execute procedures locally.

share The action a server machine performs to allow some or all of its file system to become available to other hosts.

shell The program used to communicate with the UNIX operating system. A local shell is one running on the local machine, and a remote shell is one that runs on the machine to which you are connected. The Bourne Shell normally generates a dollar sign ($) prompt to show that it is ready to accept a command.

suspend To halt temporarily a running program. A suspended program can be resumed at any time at exactly the point where it left off.

User Datagram Protocol (UDP)
A simple datagram protocol layered directly above the Internet Protocol (IP).

user identification number (UID)
A number that identifies a user to the operating system. Every user has a unique number that identifies that user to the operating system.

verifier Information used to prove that credentials are valid.

Index

Files

.cshrc 92
.dir 116
.pag 116
.profile 92
.rhosts 92
/dev/tcp 96
/dev/zero 96
/etc 43
  ASCII map files 114
  automounter maps 123, 124
  NIS maps 136
  NIS maps in 114
  ypinit termination, and 132
/etc.ypinit 116
/etc/dfs/dfstab 15, 17, 30, 36, 76
/etc/dfs/sharetab 11, 28, 36
/etc/hosts.equiv 92, 103
/etc/master.d/kernel 115, 121
/etc/mnttab 30, 31, 58
/etc/profile 72
/etc/publickey 77, 121, 122, 123, 125, 127
/etc/rc2.d/s75ppc 115
/etc/rc2.d/s75rpc 121, 134
/etc/vfstab 19, 21, 22, 23, 30, 35, 38, 41, 42, 56, 59, 76
/sbin/init.d/nfs 32
/sbin/rc3.d 30
/tmp_mnt 42, 56, 57
/usr/lib/netsvc/yp/ypbind 134
/usr/lib/netsvc/yp/ypserv 131, 152
/usr/sbin 9, 14, 15
/usr/sbin/udpublickey 123
/usr/sbin/ypinit 129
/var/yp
  domain name in 146
  in s5 file system 120, 137
  makefile in 125, 130, 139
  NIS domain maps 115
  NIS maps 116
  NIS maps in 114
  subdirectory with domain name 131
/var/yp/aliases 120, 127
/var/yp/Makefile 136, 142, 144
/var/yp/updaters 123
/var/yp/ypxfr.log 141

A

abort 153
absolute symbolic link 60
anon, option to NFS share command 17
asterisk xiii
attribute caching 20
authentication
  RPC 70
  UNIX 71
automount daemon 41, 43
automounter
  changes to a direct map 58
  debugging 58–61
  default mount point 57
  distributed files 123
  hierarchical mount 49, 59
  invoking 56–58
  mountpoint not a directory 59
  multiple mounts 48
  nullifying entry in master map 57
  overriding entry in master map 57
  required map unavailable 59
  specifying arguments in master map 57
  time out 61
automounter map 43–55
  comment in 44
  direct map 43
  distributing 55
  duplicate entry 59
  forcing changes to take effect 58

formatting 43
indirect map 43
master map 43
modifying 58
multi-line entry 44
name including colon 43
name including white space 44
option specified in indirect map 48
using environment variables 55
using substitution 53–54
writing a direct map 46–47
writing a master map 44
writing an indirect map 47–48
awk 136, 142

B

backing-up files 5
backslash xiii, 12
binding 153
biod daemons 29, 30, 32, 38
restarting 39
booting
in single user mode 78
problems 78
Bourne Shell 155
browsing available resources 24–25
BSD semantics 20

C

caller process 153
cat 136
chkey 77, 122, 123, 136
client 2, 153
client/server model 1–2
command line
broken 12
comment, in automounter file 44
crash 5
client 82, 85
server 82, 85
credential 73, 153
credentials 70
crontab 116, 139, 140, 141

D

daemon 153
killing 38
runaway 38
Data Encryption Standard, see DES
dbm
file 114, 116, 137, 142
file format 125
DES 153
DES authentication 71–72
dfmounts 25, 28
dfshares 24–25, 36
dfstab file
modifying 15
used as input to shareall 12
when read 15
diagnostics
automounter problems 58–61
fixing hung NFS programs 36
NFS client problems 35
NFS mounting problems 35–36
NFS server problems 33–34
direct map, *see* automounter map
diskless client 2, 15, 41, 78
displaying shared resources 25–26
dollar sign 55
domain 153
name 75
dropping packets 39
dynamic mounts, disabling 56

E

environment variable 55
error message, mount 35–36
example
auto.direct map 124

auto.master map 123
automatic mounting of directory 23
bringing master server to run level supporting NIS services 131
characters that might confuse automounter 43
chkey session 122
comment line in map entry 44
commenting a share command 12
default makefile 125
granting different privileges to clients 12
hard mounting resources read-write 21
hierarchical mount 50
indirect map 48
limiting a client to read-only access 12
limiting superuser access 17
listing currently available resources 25
master map 45
mounting a remote resource 2
multi-line map entry 44
name with white space 44
NIS map built from standard input 137
requesting information 25
rpcbind output 149
selective file sharing 3
sharing a resource with all clients 11
soft mounting resources read-only 21
transferring NIS map file 151
ypxfr shell script 140

F

fcntl() 81, 85
file handle 153
file hierarchy, overlapping 4
file sharing,peer-to-peer 3
file system 2
file transfer
aborting 99
getting a listing of remote files 97
preparing the connection 95, 97
quitting 99
using ftp 97
finger 109–??
formatting conventions xiii–xiv
ftp 94, 94–100

G

get 97
GID 5, 20, 154
grep 142
group identification number, see GID
grpid 20

H

hierarchy 154
host 154
hung 154
machine 37
part way through boot 38
process 20
program 33, 36, 37
hyphen 13

I

indirect map, *see* automounter map
init 8, 38
IP 156

J

job control shell 105

K

key
common 73
conversation 72, 74
names xiv

public 71, 72
secret 71, 72
keylogin 72, 78
keylogout 78
keyserv 76
keyserver 72, 73
KLM_CANCEL 85
KLM_LOCK 85
KLM_TEST 85
KLM_UNLOCK 85

L

link,untouched 43
local machine 154
lock manager, seeNetwork Lock Manager
lockd 82
lockf() 81, 85
login 78
ls 96, 97

M

make 116, 125, 130, 136
makedbm 114, 116, 120, 130, 136–138
map file 42, 154
equivalent entries 56
mapname.dir 114
mapname.pag 114
master map, *see* automounter map
metacharacter
* 98
? 98
shell 92
mget 98
mknod 96
mount 154
mount 18–21, 37, 42, 43
debugging NFS problems 35–36
intr option 21
nosuid option 21
specific options 19–21
with bg option 33
mount point 19, 154
creating 19
local 2
mount process 29–31
mountall 30
mountd daemon 28, 30, 31, 35
mounting resources 18–23
from the command line 30–31
read-only 45
remote 2
setting number of retries 20
setting read buffer size 20
setting server's IP port number 20
setting timeout 20
setting timeout period 20
setting write buffer size 20
mput 98
MS-DOS 1

N

netstat 39
network
bad connection 38
small 55
Network File System, *see* NFS
Network Lock Manager 5, 81–86
Network Status Monitor 82
newkey 77, 122, 123, 136
NFS 154
about 1
administration 6
advantages 4–6
booting and setuid problems 78
checking status 63
compatibility with pre-3.0 versions 28
error messages 35–36
file sharing model 1–4
installing 7–8
machine maintenance 6
menu interface, see sysadm

operation 8
starting 63
starting and stopping 8
starting and stopping from the command line 8
stopping 63
tracking down problems 31–39

NFS resources
defined xi
granting root access 17
hard mounted 33
hard mounting 18, 21
mounting 18–21
mounting automatically 18
obtaining information 23–26
soft mounted 33, 37
soft mounting 18, 21
unmounting see also umount

NFS_GETFH system call 31

nfsd daemons 28–29, 31, 32, 36
determining if running 37

NIS binding
network load 119
overview 119

NIS client
debugging 145–149
described 118
ensuring that slave server uses NIS 132
hung 146–147
preparing to configure 121
setting up 134

NIS domain
adding a new NIS server 143
assignment to 115
described 115
establishing 120–121
maintaining maps in 135
naming 121
preparing 120
using crontab to update slave servers 140

NIS machine types 117

NIS maps
adding to makefile 142
administering 135–145
auto.direct 124, 128, 129, 133
auto.home 124, 128, 129, 133
auto.master 123, 128, 129, 133, 135, 139
building with ypinit 129
built from standard input 137–138
changing master server, and 144–145
copies on slave server 117
creating 136
creating from keyboard 137
default 115
described 114
modifying standard maps 136
on NIS server 117
propagating 139–141
propagating to slave server 133
setting up client machine 134
updating 135–138
updating from existing ASCII files 137
ypserv disabled and map updates 152

NIS master server
choosing 117, 118
creating new slave server 132
domain name 131, 146
map files 142
modifying NIS maps 136
propagating maps to slave servers 116
restricting access 130

NIS server
described 117–118
temporary 141

NIS service 132
debugging 145–152

implementing 120–134
unavailable 147–148
NIS slave server 131, 132, 139, 142–143, 151
nobody 10, 16, 17

P

passwd file 96
peripheral 2
ping 110–111
failure 60
process identification number 155
public key cryptography 71, 121, 155
publickey 77, 136, 139
publickey.byname 115
publickey.dir 127
publickey.pag 127
publickey.time 127, 128
put 97

R

rcp 88–92, 132
redirection characters 93
remote file copy, see rcp
remote files, slow access 38
remote machine 155
Remote Procedure Call, *see* RPC
remount failure 61
resource 155
peer-to-peer sharing 4
resource, see alsoNFS resource
rlogin 78, 87, 92, 102–106
root access 18
security implications 11
RPC 2, 6, 28, 31, 72, 82, 153, 155
authentication 70
utilities 8
RPC authentication 70
RPC/XDR 82
rpcbind 30, 34, 35, 148
rpcinfo 34
rsh 92–94
run level 130, 132, 134, 155
checking 35
run level 2 131
run level 3 8, 15, 18, 21, 28, 29, 35, 36, 58

S

s5 file system 120, 127, 137
secure NFS 5, 20, 69–79
administering 75–77
administring /etc/publickey with NIS 121
secure RPC 70–75, 121, 122
client/server session 72–75
security
attacks on 69
sed 136, 142
server 1, 155
crash 78
server crash, and hierarchical mount 50
server failure
recovery from 5
server not responding 33
server process 155
set-gid bits 19
set-uid bits 19
setuid problems, NFS 78
share 9, 9–12, 25
secure option 10
specific options 10–11, 16
shareall 9, 12–14, 30
sharing files 155
sharing resources 9–18
allowing root access 10
as-needed 9
automatic 9, 15–16
from the command line 9
in a trusting environment 18
on a regular basis 15
overiding ro for selected clients 10
overriding rw for selected clients 10
read-only 10

- read-write 10
- requiring user authentication 10
- stopping 14, 15

sharing special device files 2
shell 155
slave server daemons, starting 133
square brackets xiii
`statd` 82, 86
`statfs` 31
superuser 16, 17, 18, 30, 33, 69, 75
- accessing resources as 16–18
- assignment to NIS domain 115
- changing master server's map 144
- creating public key map 122
- modifying NIS maps 136
- naming NIS domain as 121

suspend 156
symbolic link 42
`sysadm` 63–68
- invoking 64
- listing remote resources 68
- listing resources shared by NFS 67
- local resource sharing 66–67
- modifying mount permissions 68
- modifying sharing permissions 67
- mounting remote resources 67–68
- setup procedure 64
- sharing local resources 67
- starting and stopping NFS 65–66
- system_setup menu 64
- unmounting resources 68
- unsharing local resources 67

System V Release 4.0 5, 7
- NIS maps, and 114
- secure networking in 121
- utilities 7

T

TCP/IP 6, 8, 87
`telnet` 78, 87, 106–108
`tftp` 94, 100–101
timestamp 74

U

UDP 6, 11, 156
UID 5, 10, 16, 75
- with value zero 17

`umount` 22, 58
UNIX System, authentication 71
unmounting resources 21
`unshare` 9, 14
`unshareall` 9, 15
User Datagram Protocol, see UDP
user identification number 156

V

verifier 70, 73, 74, 156
vertical bar xiii
VMS 1

Y

`ypbind` 119, 134
- communication with `ypserv` 146
- crashes 148–149
- defined 115
- port numbers 152

`ypcat` 116, 144, 148
`ypfiles` 114
`ypinit`
- adding new NIS server 143
- establishing NIS domain 120
- NIS database 116
- NIS map files 135
- setting the master server with 129–134
- updating NIS maps 138

`ypmake` 117
`ypmaster` 151
`ypmatch` 116
`yppoll` 116, 148
`yppush`

notification of new NIS map 151
obtaining initial copy of NIS map 142
propagating an NIS map 139
propagating data to slave servers 116, 127
use when changing map's master server 144

ypserv
call to ypxfr 116
changes to upon rebooting 152
crash 152
defined 115
hung client 147
NIS binding 119
NIS server overloaded 146
propagating an NIS map 139
setting slave servers 132
starting daemons in the master server 130

ypservers 116, 139, 143, 151
ypset 116, 147
ypslave 151
ypupdated 115, 122, 123
ypwhich 116, 119, 146, 147, 149
ypxfr
called by ypinit 132
changing a map's master server with 144, 145
described 116
directly invoking 141
logging activities 141
problem with NIS server map 151
propagating an NIS map 139–141
using shell scripts with 140

Notes

Notes

Notes

Notes

Notes

Notes

Notes

Notes

Notes

Notes

Notes

Notes

Notes

Notes